The Indians of North Florida

From Carolina to Florida, the Story of the Survival of a Distinct American Indian Community

Christopher Scott Sewell
and
S. Pony Hill

Backintyme
Palm Coast, Florida, U.S.A.

Backintyme Publishing
30 Medford Drive
Palm Coast FL 32137-2504

860-468-9631
website: http://backintyme.com/publishing.php
email: sales@backintyme.com

Printed in the United States of America
June 2011

ISBN: 9780939479375
Library of Congress Control Number: 2011905360

The free negroes in this county are mixed-blood, almost white and are intermarried with a low class of whites – Have no trade, occupation or profession they live in a settlement or Town of their own their personal property consists of Cattle and Hogs, They make no produce except corn and peas and very little of that, They are a lazy Indolent and worthless race.

— 1860 Federal Census of Calhoun County narrative concerning Scott's Ferry

There are men who would knife us out of having our own school saying that we are negroe. You know our character that we are of white and Indian blood.

— Scotts Ferry School Trustee Dave Martin to Calhoun County Clerk of Court,1938

Some of the forefathers claim there was no negro blood, but there was Indian blood. This, we are unable to substantiate by any official records.

— JD Milton, Superintendent of Jackson County Schools in correspondence upon interviewing Tom Scott of Scott Town as to the community's origins-1942

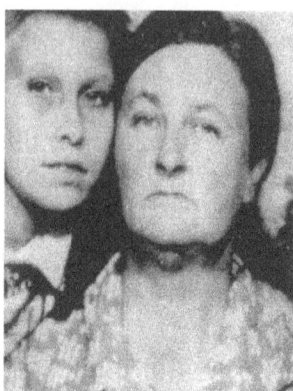

Table of Contents

CHERAW SURNAMES LIST VII

NOTE TO THE READER IX

INTRODUCTION 1

1. "A VERY LARGE NATION" THE COLONIAL PERIOD .. 5

2. "FORCED, IN A MEASURE" THE MULATTO LABEL .. 19

3. "A COMPANY OF FRIENDLY INDIANS" THE FLORIDA FRONTIER 27

4. "ALL OF WHOM CLAIM TO BE CATAWBAS" THE FLORIDA CATAWBA 41

5. "A MOTLEY CREW OF HALF-BREED INDIANS" THE CIVIL WAR 53

6. "A SETTLEMENT OR TOWN OF THEIR OWN" SCOTT'S FERRY 59

7. "A LARGE PERCENTAGE OF INDIAN BLOOD" SCOTT TOWN 83

8. "LIKE OTHER GOOD INDIANS" THE WOODS COMMUNITY 97

9. "CLAIM TO BE PART SPANISH AND INDIAN" OTHER FLORIDA GROUPS OF CHERAW ANCESTRY 127

APPENDIX 149

Cheraw Surnames List

Using oral history interviews from tribal elders of several panhandle communities, voluminous federal and state census records, Civil War Veteran Pension applications, WWI Civil enlistments, WWII records, Holmes, Walton, Liberty, Calhoun and Jackson County School Records and correspondences, Cherokee Indian Normal School (Pembroke NC) records, and countless historical, reference, and index books from the Florida State Archives, I have compiled a list of *some* of the surnames associated with the 3 central panhandle communities (Scott Town, Scotts Ferry, and Woods), as well as the Walton and Holmes counties Cheraw/Euchee ancestry settlements known as the Dominickers. Most of these families trace to Carolina Cheraw roots but some also have Catawba, Cherokee, Creek, Lumbee, and even Pamunkey Indian ancestry as the research shows so far. Most of these surnames are found among the students who attended the Indian schools that were funded as Colored in the early twentieth century in Calhoun and Jackson Counties, Florida, some of which are found in the appendix.

Surnames of Documented Cheraw (Catawba, Lumbee, etc) /Creek Ancestry:

- Ammons
- Ayers
- Barnwell
- Bass
- Bennett
- Bird
- Blanchard
- Boggs
- Brown
- Bullard
- Bunch
- Bryant
- Brooks
- Chason
- Chavis
- Conyers
- Copeland
- Davis
- Doyle
- Goins
- Hall
- Harris
- Hicks
- Hill
- Holly
- Ireland
- Jacobs
- Johnson
- Jones
- Kever
- Laramore
- Linton
- Lollie
- Lolly
- Long
- Lovett
- Mainer
- Martin
- Mayo
- Moses
- Oxendine
- Perkins
- Porter
- Potter
- Revels
- Rollin
- Scott
- Simmons
- Smith
- Stafford
- Stephens
- Sweat
- Thomas
- Whitfield
- William

Note to the Reader

In this text the term *Cheraw* is used to describe the remnants of large Eastern Siouan tribes who did and still do live in the Carolinas. The terms *Cheraw Indians of north Florida, Florida Catawba, Florida Cheraw, Cheraw-Catawba,* etc. are used to describe some families of these Indians who had moved to Florida from the Carolinas and settled in the early 1800's.

In the same time period that such families as Scott, Oxendine, Jacobs, Hill, Conyers, Copeland, Bullard, Bass, Johnson, Blanchard, Brown, Moses, Long, Hicks, Barnwell, Stephens, Chavis, Bunch and many other Indian families from the Carolinas were settling the areas that would become Scott Town, Scotts Ferry, and Blountstown, the historic Apalachicola Creek Indians were being removed from the Florida panhandle to Texas and Indian Territory by the federal government as part of the forced removal of the Five Civilized Tribes that occurred during the 1830's. Various bands of Muskogee-speaking Indians were removed or harassed into other areas during this period.

As for the Indians living in Blountstown, they were one of many groups within the larger Creek Nation's confederacy of tribal towns, (half of which spoke tribal languages other than Muskogee). The Apalachicola Creek Indian Reservation at Blountstown headed by Chief John

Blount, an Alabama Indian, as well as 4 other Creek reservations in the panhandle were terminated in the 1830's and the people were soon removed to the west. The Apalachicola Indians from the John Blount Reservation on the Apalachicola River (today's Blountstown) were removed to the Alabama tribal territory in eastern Texas, where John Blount's uncle, Red Shoes was Head Chief. According to all available documentary evidence the extent of the social relationship between the in-migrating Carolina Cheraw Indians and the departing Apalachicola Creeks is unknown.

Oral histories within particular Blountstown Indian families speak of intermarriage with individual Apalachicola Creeks who did not go on the removal. No documentary evidence has yet come to light to substantiate the large amounts of oral history within certain Blountstown Indian families substantiating these claimed events. The degree of social interaction during the late 1830's and 40's between departing Apalachicola Creeks and recently arriving Cheraw (Lumbee, Catawba and other Carolina Siouan stock) Indians is as yet unknown, but to date there is no documentary archival evidence of a remnant Apalachicola Creek Indian population remaining in the Jackson, Calhoun, or Liberty Counties area, though there are many descendants of other Creek tribal groups who moved to the area. Some of these Creek families, like the Hill, Holly, and other families, did migrate to Florida from areas of the southeast that had formerly been in or near the Old Creek Nation, mostly from in or near South Carolina from the documentary records indications.

Upon coming to Florida, some of these migrating Creeks did marry into the Cheraw's settlements already established there, as with the Hill family. Some of these hybrid families and those already in the settlements were the roots of the established Indian settlements like Scott Town and others. This is a different social situation from the tens, if not hundreds of thousands of descendants of removal era Creek Indians who remained. The descendants of those remnant Creeks are everywhere in the south, and were socially treated as White, not Colored, under Jim Crow segregation.

Introduction

Over the past twenty years, my cousin, Steven Pony Hill and I have compiled records, interviewed elders, and spent hundreds if not thousands of hours in the Florida State Archives and in a dozen or so courthouse records rooms across the panhandle. This has been a search to find out the documentary history of our people. The search was encouraged and supported by our elders and community members, elders who told us the rich oral history of our people. It is a story that we found to be very different when viewed from the outside, viewed from the perspective of non-Indians who wrote about us, knew our ancestors, and who controlled the institutions of the society that surrounded us. We found it a dark time, when we stayed as insulated within our own community as possible. Ancestors who we knew to be Indians from our grandparent's stories and personal recollections, to our surprise the historic records called other names like Mulatto, Negros, Dominickers, and White.

What continues to emerge as the endless work of documenting our history through the records of the dominant mainstream society is a steady confrontation with challenges to our survival as a group of people, a community, legally, socially, and spiritually. This is a struggle that from the very beginnings of our identity as a unique people on the American scene many centuries ago to our contemporary fight for a place in the America of the twenty first century, we have won, if only by our continued survival.

The story of the Cheraw Indians of north Florida, a tribal people who have lived in the Apalachicola and Chipola River valleys of Florida for nearly two hundred years, is a long and circuitous one. Though far from having the large populations of the past two centuries, today there are still many individuals and families living in several historic rural hamlets. Since the 1950's, the heart of this tribal community is Blountstown, in Calhoun County, the center of Indian political life for the past 60 years. The 3 historic settlements addressed in this narrative were once population strongholds during the segregation era (1860-1960). The settlements of Scott Town, in Jackson County, Woods in Liberty County, and Scott's Ferry, in Calhoun County, despite being located in separate counties, all are fairly near to each other geographically, with Scott's Ferry and Woods separated by the Apalachicola River.

As with all communities, times changed and by the end of the 1950's, many families were already relocating to Blountstown, Marianna, and other areas, near and far. The history of The Cheraw Indians of North Florida can be divided into three distinct time periods:

- 1800-1860, the time of migration to Florida by Cheraw and Creek families through to the Civil War
- 1860-1960, the Civil War to the end of segregation (the Civil Rights era)
- 1960-present, the post-segregation era and struggles for tribal government, infrastructure, and State and Federal acknowledgement.

Each time period in the story of The Cheraw Indians of North Florida has its own unique challenges and adaptations by the people to the pressures of the day.

In the beginning the colonial frontier was a wild and rough place, and the situations in the Carolinas of the times led the first few families to migrate to Spanish Florida. Many were successful and the establishment of Indian hamlets at Scott Town and Scott's Ferry led to a thriving and unique way of life for the people. This can be seen in the census and tax records of the times that show that the pre-conflict Scotts Ferry was one of the most thriving communities in the county. The documentary evidence for Scott Town shows a similar situation there, with the people of the Indian settlements listed as Free Persons of Color (as distinct from Free Negro) on the census and doing well.

With the coming of the conflict between the north and south the situation would change, and a new social reality would unfold. In the years before the Civil war, one's status as a slave or descendent of a slave, or as a free person would be the main mechanism defining social status.

In the dark days after the War Between the States, skin color came to be a determining factor of one's social standing, and a new era of unrestricted racism began.

In this text I hope to shine a small amount of light on what has been the journey of a unique people so far, and a story of survival. There is still much research to be done. One hopes that the younger generations of The Cheraw Indians of North Florida will support the ongoing struggle to strengthen the community by participating in the life of the tribal community.

Willie Porter (son of Mathias) and
Lumbee Indian Beasley Bullard

The girls are all daughters of Willie Copeland and Bessie
Porter

1. "A Very Large Nation" The Colonial Period

Little is known about the Catawba Tribe prior to their first encounters with Europeans. They were known to the Cherokee as *Ani-Suwa'li* (the Suwali people). The Catawba Tribe was actually a loose confederation of tribes who all spoke a version of the Siouan language. Known by such general names as the Cheroenhaka, Esaw, Isaw, Sara, and Saraw, this confederacy of eastern Siouan peoples included the Kadapau, Sugaree, Coree, Coharie, Manahoac, Hassinunga, Shakori, Eno, Occaneechi, Saponi, and Tutelo. Encountering them in 1701, explorer John Lawson described them as "the Esaw Indians, a very large Nation, containing many thousands of people."

In the early 1600's many important historic incidents happened, which would affect the Catawba descendants for generations to come. Already suffering from constant raids from the Iroquois and Tuscarora on their northern border, and the Cherokee to the west, the Catawba now faced a new threat, European colonists pushing inland from the east. Catawba Indians being taken captive by raiding parties of Iroquois and Cherokee were being sold as slaves to the colonists and this did nothing to better the situation. From 1616 to 1630, Opechancanough, successor of

Powhatan, and chief over all the Algonquin speaking tidewater tribes, expressed his displeasure with the encroaching White men by waging a bloody war. Indian captives were taken in increasing numbers from the tidewater tribes during this time and forced into slavery. Those Indians not taken as slaves were forced to wander the Maryland, Virginia, and Carolina area. In 1657 the English forced most of the Powhatan remnants onto reservations in Virginia and the Siouan tribes were gathered in four main concentrations:

> The Monacan, along the James; the Saponi along the Rivana and James Rivers and Otter Creek; the Tutelo in the Roanoke Valley; and the Occaneechi on islands at the confluence of the Roanoke and Dan Rivers.

Arguably the most influential event to occur in the 1600's happened in 1660 when Virginia determined that "...an Indian sold by another Indian or an Indian who speaks English and who desires baptism will now receive his or her freedom." This allowed many Algonquin and Siouan war captives held in slavery in the colonies to regain their freedom, but it also provided incentive for their masters to downplay the Indian ancestry of those in servitude in order to retain them. These former slaves quickly rejoined their tribesmen bringing with them their acquired skills as carpenters, wheelwrights, and ferry operators. Most importantly, these newly freed Indians brought with them their new English names and Christian religion. Unfortunately they also retained the stigma of being former slaves, a condition which would cause their White neighbors to eye them with suspicion for generations.

In 1713, the confederated eastern Siouan Nations signed a Treaty of Peace with the Virginia Colonial government at Williamsburg. Among the different Nations represented were the Occaneechi, the Stuckanok, the Tottero, and the Saponi. At the invitation of Governor Spottswood of Virginia, these Indians settled a four-square-mile reservation encompassing the north and south side of the Meherrin River. On the north banks were the Nansemond and related Algonquin-speaking bands, on the south were the Siouan-speaking Tutelo, Saponi, Cheroenhaka, Eno, a small band of Catawba, and also an Iroquoian-speaking band of Tuscarora who had avoided the war with the Carolina settlers just 2 years earlier. Spottswood endorsed the construction of Fort Christanna where the Indian children had mandatory training in academics and Christianity. After the closing of the Fort Christanna School a few of the students followed headmaster Charles Griffin and enrolled at the Brafferton Indian School at William and Mary.

Because of the continued hostilities between these Nations and the Iroquois to the north, the governors of New York, Pennsylvania, and Virginia held a conference at Albany in September of 1722 to hammer out a peaceable agreement between the Tribes on their borders. Governor Spottswood undertook negotiations for the Christanna Indians who were composed of the "Saponies, Ochineeches, Stenkenoaks, Meipontskys, and Toteroes."

In addition to their traditional native enemies, it is obvious that the remnant tribes considered the encroaching White settlements as an almost equal threat. It also appears that, on the subject of trespassing Whites, even the Algonquin and Siouan peoples could agree and cooperate. On October 24, 1723 the Virginia Government spoke out on behalf of the Meherrin and Nansemond Nations and warned the North Carolinians:

> Whereas, the Maherin and Nansemond Indians have this day complained that notwithstanding the repeated orders of this government for security to them the possession of their lands, whereon they have many years past been seated, between the Nottoway and Maherine Rivers, divers persons under pretense of grants from the

Government of North Carolina surveyed the lands of
the said Indians and begun to make settlements within
their cleared grounds.

This report is especially interesting as it implies that
portions of the Nansemond had obviously moved west of
their ancestral homes around Norfolk, Virginia, and were
living with the Meherrin between the Nottoway and Meherrin Rivers. Peace with the tribes to the north allowed the
remnant Eastern Sioux to live in peace and relative obscu-
rity for several years. All was not completely serene, however, as a letter to the governor from one R. Everand, a settler living near the Meherrin Indians, refers to disturbances
involving the Meherrins and Nottoways in 1727. Everand
says that the Meherrins denied any attacks on the Nottoways, stating, "they lay the whole blame upon the old
Occaneechy King and the Saponi Indians."

It is evident that Virginia continued to trade with
these Nations and found the trade relations lucrative
enough to employ an interpreter to the Saponi and Occaneechi Indians as late as 1730. After 1730, a group of
Saponi undertook one of many trips south to take up residence among the Catawba. Conditions must not have been
to their liking, as they soon returned to the Virginia-North
Carolina border accompanied by some Cheraws. Upon arriving at their old lands between the Roanoke and Meherrin, they petitioned Lt. Governor Gooch for permission to
resettle in Virginia, which was granted in 1733.

Possibly because of the inability to possess commu-
nal lands, or most likely because of acculturation, it is apparent that the eastern Siouan remnants began to live as
individual landowners during the 1730 to 1740 period. It is
also during this period that land deeds begin appearing under the names of such Other Free Persons surnames as
Scott, Chavis, Goings, Bunch, Collins, and Gibson. With
each new land patents by a concentration of these families,

a report of eastern Siouan people would be generated. For example, after William Chavis, Thomas Parker, Gideon Gibson, and Henry Bunch recorded their land grants on the Eno River in Orange County, North Carolina adjoining the lands of William Eaton, a report from the Colonial Records of NC identifies a group of 30 to 40 Saponi had settled on the lands of William Eaton. The Siouan identity of these persons is further bolstered by reports such as one originating in Orange County in 1742 regarding some Saponi Indians accused of hog stealing:

> Alexander Macharton, John Bowling, Manicassa, Captain Tom, Isaac, Harry, Blind Tom, Foolish Jack, Charles Griffin, John Collins, Little Jack, Indians, giving security for good behaviour.

Governor Clarence Gooch of Virginia reported to the Colonial Office for the years 1743 to 1747 that the, "Saponies and other petty nations associated with them…are retired out of Virginia to the Cattawbas."

This time period corresponds to the appearance of such English surnames as Harris, Stephens, Scott, Brown, and Canty among the Catawba. A 1761 report counted 20 Saponi warriors in the area of Granville County, NC and this corresponds to the Mulatto, Mustee or Indian taxation in Granville of such families as Anderson, Jeffries, Davis, Chavis, Going, Bass, Harris, Brewer, Bunch, Griffin, Pettiford, Evans, and others in the 1760's.

In 1757, the Virginia governor at Williamsburg received a delegation of Indians including "King Blunt and the thirty-three Tuscaroras, seven Meherrins, two Saponies and thirteen Nottoways."

This date corresponds to military and land records of free persons of color such as William Allen, Adam Ivey, James Evans, Benjamin Chavis, Allen Sweat, James Jones and Isham Scott who were residing in the ancestral Siouan areas of Halifax County, NC along the banks of the Roanoke River. John R. Swanton also reports that the Meherrin Indians:

> Were living on Roanoke River in 1781 with the southern bands of Tuscarora and Saponi, and the Machapunga.

In addition to the Siouan people, there were also remnants of Algonquin tribes residing in the North Carolina-Virginia border country. Near Norfolk, in the Dismal Swamp area, resided a remnant of the Nansemond Nation. On July 15, 1833 the Quality Superior Court of Norfolk County entered the following minutes:

> The Court doth certify upon satisfactory evidence of white persons Produced before it, that Asa Price, Wright Perkins, Nathan Perkins, Pricilla Perkins, Nelson Bass, Willis Bass, Andrew Bass, William Bass son of William Bass, Joseph Newton, and Henry Newton, and Allen Newton, Polly Newton, Sally Newton, and Hestor Newton are not free-Negroes or Mulattoes, but are of Indian descent and that each of them have a certificate separately thereof.

Again on July 20, 1833, the same Court again addressed the issue of certain persons' race:

> The Court doth certify upon satisfactory evidence of white persons Produced before it that Andrew Bass and Lavina his wife, Elizabeth Bass wife of William Bass son of William Bass, Jemima Bass Sr., Peggy Bass, Jemima Bass Jr., Elizabeth Lidwin, Mary Anderson, Priscilla Flury, Jerusha Bass the wife of William the son of Willis, Frances the wife of James Newton, Lucy Trummel wife of William Trummel, Andrew Bass Jr., Patsy Bass, William Bass, William Newton, Betsy Weaver, Nancy Weaver, and Sally Weaver, that they are not Free Negroes or Mulattoes, but are of Indian descent and that each of them have a certificate separately thereof.

These two reports are quite significant in the documentation of the eastern Siouan people, as the Bass, Anderson, Perkins, and Weaver surnames appear frequently among the mixed-blood communities spread from Virginia to Florida. Just south of the Nansemond of Norfolk, across the border in Chowan County, what remained of the Chowan Nation were still very much present. In 1724, a total of 11,360 acres was set aside for the Chowan Indians near Bennett's Creek. Over the years the large Chowan reservation was chipped away as the Indians sold small tracts to satisfy debts and otherwise provide for the tribal needs. In 1734 James Bennett, Thomas Hoyter, Charles Beasley, Jeremiah Purkins (probably Perkins), John Robbins, John Reading (probably Reed), and Nuce Will, "Chief men of the Chowan Indians," sold land on Bennett's Creek in the part of Chowan County which later became Gates County.

In 1758, "James Bennett, John Robbins, Chief men of the Chowan Indians" sold 300 acres of Indian land by deed proved in Gates County, and again in 1763 there appears a record of "James Bennett, James Bennett jr., Amos Bennett, being Bennett's Creek Indians" sold land acknowledged in Chowan County Court. Though a clear record existed to support the Chowans' continued claim to their land, this did not stop several local White land speculators from attempting to uproot them.

In 1790 a petition was submitted from Gates County to the North Carolina Legislature, which read:

> The petitioners request the legislature to pass a law validating acquisition by a group of descendants of Indians and blacks. In 1724 the Chowan Indians received 11,360 acres of land in Chowan County, later Gates County. The Indians sold most of the land. The Indian men all died, and the women mixed with Negroes. The free blacks and their mixed-blood children served as

soldiers for the colonials in the Revolution. Supported by William Lewis, Samuel Harrell, and other white men, they seek title to small remnants of the aforesaid tract of land.

Disguised as an attempt by charitable citizens to assist a poor, desolate people, was a dark conspiracy to liquidate any future land claim by these descendants of the Chowan Nation. Asserting that the Indian men had died and the women had mixed with Negroes served two purposes; first claiming that all the Indian men had died would effectively negate the land title, and second, claiming Negro ancestry for the group would deny them further legal recourse. Records clearly prove a direct male descendant line from the James Bennett, John Robbins, Jeremiah Perkins, and John Reed of 1734 to many of the families mentioned in 1790, yet this glaring fact was ignored.

Censused as part of this community of Chowan Indian descendants in 1790 were the Reed, Robbins, Blanchard, Bennett, Cuff, Weaver, Mitchell, and Hunter families, surnames which had already begun appearing in other mixed-blood communities before 1790. Military, land, and tax records reveal that the eastern Siouan remnant families continued to concentrate their settlements in their ancestral lands around the Eno, Tar, Roanoke, Meherrin, and Nottaway Rivers at the border of North Carolina and Virginia. In addition to these settlements and the well-known one on the Catawba reservation, other smaller bands had also spread further into Virginia, south to the Drowning Creek area of mid-southern NC, and along the Wateree and Pee Dee Rivers of South Carolina. Referring to Indians in Virginia in 1763, Lt. Governor Francis Fauquier wrote to the Lords Commissioners of Trade and Plantation Affairs that:

> There are some of the Nottoways, Meherrins, Tuscaroras, and Saponys, who tho' they live in peace in the

midst of us, lead in great measure the lives of wild Indians.

The North and South Carolina border became a favored haunt of the Eastern Sioux as early as the 1730's. In addition to the previously mentioned Saponi retired out of Virginia to the Cattawbas, a band of Cheraw brokered a deal with Welsh Baptist settlers from Delaware for land in present-day Marlboro County. A large group of Nottoway, numbering about 300, was reported on "the northern frontiers of South Carolina between 1748 and 1754." Beginning in the 1790's many of these families from the Roanoke area began to assert their Indian ancestry in courts across South Carolina. In 1794, the South Carolina Legislature received a petition from Isaac Linagear, Isaac Mitchell, Jonathan Price, Spencer Bolton, William N. Sweat, and 29 other free persons of color seeking to repeal the Act for imposing a poll tax on all free Negroes, mustees, and mulatoes. On April 6, 1832 a certificate was issued to South Carolina resident Sarah G. Jacobs, which cancelled her requirement to submit to the free Negro tax, and included the fact that "she appears to be of Indian descent."

A petition to the Legislature in 1859 inquiring whether "persons of Indian descent are considered to be free persons of color and liable for the poll tax," caused a determination that Frederick Chavis, Lewis Chavis, Durany Chavis, James Jones, Mary Jones, and Jonathan Williams, "do not qualify under the term 'free person of color' as they are of Indian ancestry."

When the Gibson family arrived in South Carolina from the Halifax area, their presence caused much of a stir. Gideon Gibson came to the attention of the South Carolina Common's House of Assembly in 1731 when a member announced in Chamber that several "free Colored men with their White wives had emigrated from Virginia with the intention of settling on the Santee River." Governor Robert

Johnson summoned Gideon and his family to explain their presence there and, after meeting them, reported:

> I have had them before me in Council and upon exami-
> nation find that they are not Negroes nor slaves but
> Free People, that the father of them here is named
> Gideon Gibson and his father was also free, I have been
> informed by a person who has lived in Virginia that this
> Gibson has lived there several years in good repute and
> by his papers that he produced before me that his trans-
> actions there have been very regular, That he has for
> several years paid taxes for two tracts of land and had
> seven Negroes of his own, That he is a carpenter by
> Trade and is come hither for the support of his fam-
> ily...I have in consideration of his wife's being a white
> woman and several white women capable of working
> and being Serviceable in the county permitted him to
> settle in this Country.

Over 30 years later, incidents would occur which would, no doubt, cause the Governor to regret his decision. Gideon's son, Gideon Gibson jr., was living on the south side of the Pee Dee River at a place called Duck Pond. On July 25, 1767, as a leader of the Regulators, Gideon was involved in a skirmish with a constable's party near Marrs Bluff on the Pee Dee. The South Carolina Gazette reported on August 15th that Gibson's band of Regulators was a:

> Gang of banditi, a numerous collection of outcast mu-
> lattos, mustees, free Negroes, etc. all horse thieves from
> the borders of Virginia and northern colonies...headed
> by one Gideon Gibson.

Henry Laurens, a prominent Charleston merchant, described Gideon Gibson in this way:

> Reasoning from the colour carries no convic-
> tion...Gideon Gibson escaped the penalties of the Ne-
> gro law by producing upon comparison more red and
> white in his face than can be discovered in the faces of

half the descendants of the French refugees in our House of Assembly.

A comparison of the Other free persons head of households who appear in the early 1800's at the NC/VA (Halifax area) border and the NC/SC (Dillon and Sumter area) border reveal an obvious parallel of eastern Siouan families. Surnames shared between these two groups include Scott, Richardson, Chavis, Clark, Going, Jones, Hathcock, Locklear, Mitchell, Sweat and Williams. There can be no denying that the South Carolina settlements are a branch of the older, ancestral settlements of the Roanoke River area. Further evidence reveals that bloodlines also spread north to previously established reservation areas in Virginia and Maryland. Northampton County, on the eastern shore of Virginia, is home to the Gingaskin Indian reservation, a parcel of over 600 acres set aside for this band of Indians.

1733 brought an in-migration of Catawba and Siouan families to the Gingaskin reservation, as reported by Lt. Governor Gooch, and these families had such surnames as Fisherman, Guy, Jeffries, Collins, Scott, Daniel, Stevens and Cross. These families joined (and intermarried with) a pre-established community of mixed White/ Portuguese/ Gingaskin Indian peoples who bore such surnames as Harmon, Webb, Bingham, Weeks, George, Driggers, Landrum, Jacobs, Carter, Pool, Lang, Francis and Moses.

With the influx of Catawba, individuals on the reservation began adopting military titles such as 'Captain' and 'Major', a phenomenon that occurred at the same time among the reservated Catawba and the Pamunkey on their King William County reservation. Some of these newly united families were not long to stay, however, and Gov. Gooch again reported in 1743 that some of them had left to rejoin the Catawba on their reservation. In 1792, the Virginia General Assembly ordered that the Gingaskin Indian

Town land be divided up. The 690-acre tract was split into 27 lots that were allocated to the surviving tribal members, among whom appeared the surname Driggers and Francis (both surnames which occurred with frequency among the 'other free persons' of Halifax, NC in 1790).

Twenty-one years earlier South Carolina Regulators reported that they had tracked a convicted felon named Winslow Driggers (who had earlier escaped from a jail in Savannah, Georgia) and captured him, near Drowning Creek, in the Charraw settlement.

By the 1850's the Driggers surname was also common among another remnant Indian group, the Nanticoke of Maryland. Interestingly enough, the Nanticoke also shared the surnames of Harmon and Clark in common with the eastern Siouan of Halifax, NC. In 1855, Levi Sockum sold powder and shot to his son-in-law Isaac Harmon. Sockum was charged with violating a law that forbade supplying firearms to Negroes and mulattoes. Harmon and Sockum both denied any Negro ancestry.

A relative of the two men, Lydia Clark, claimed to be the last full-blood Nanticoke. She testified that Harmon's ancestor was an enslaved African who had married his mistress. The half-breed offspring of this union, Lydia Clark testified, had intermarried with some of the remaining Nanticoke. Judge George Fisher, who had prosecuted Harmon and Sockum, later wrote an article for a newspaper in 1895. Fisher reminisced that Harmon was:

> A young man, of perfectly Caucasian features, dark
> chestnut brown hair, rosy cheeks and hazel eyes; and by
> odds the handsomest man in the courtroom, and yet he
> was alleged to be a mulatto.

After peace was made between the Virginia tribes and their ancient enemy, the Iroquois in 1722, a band of Siouans traveled north and settled on the Susquehanna at Shamokin, Pensylvania, under Iroquois protection. Their chiefs were allowed to sit in the great council of the Six Nations, and the political status of the tribe was described as that of "a prop or support, between the logs in the wall of the Long House." In 1771 these eastern Sioux, now lumped together under the name of Tutelo, were settled on the east side of Cayuga inlet, about 3 miles from the south end of the lake. In the 1880's, Horatio Hale interviewed Nikonha whom he described as the last full-blood Tutelo living among the Iroquois. Nikonha informed Hale that his Tutelo name was Washinga and gave Hale lengthy description of the Tutelo dialect, which upon later examination, proved to be clearly Siouan and closely related to the Catawba language. Nikonha died in 1871.

2. "Forced, in a measure" The Mulatto Label

For the last 200 years numerous Indian descendants have been fighting a legal, and often racially charged, battle due to historical and modern-day race classification. The dreaded historical beast of southeastern Indian communities that continues to rear its ugly head is the fact that from the mid 1700's to after 1900 most Indian groups or individuals east of the Mississippi were racially classified as Mulatto. The reasons and justifications for this are rooted deeply in the history of southern slavery, land ownership, and political power.

Prior to 1850 the federal census and most county tax books only distinguished 4 types of persons; free White males, free White females, free persons of color, and slaves. By the record keeping of the time Indians not taxed were not supposed to be recorded at all. These non-taxed Indians assumedly lived on reservations and therefore were not required to be subject to federal census or county tax recordings. However, the inhabitants of many state reservations and some federal Indian land grants were recorded on these documents. In 1705 the Virginia Legislature passed into law that the offspring of an Indian and a White is a Mulatto.

This law went on to state that if the half-Indian Mulatto was to marry a White person then that Mulatto and his or her offspring were to be legally regarded as White (this is undoubtedly where the notion arose that a person should be of at least ¼ blood to be considered an Indian).

The Virginians were using the word *Mulatto* in its historical usage, from the root word *mule*, meaning any crossbreed. With the independent formation of the lower southern states, each state adopted racial classifications roughly equivalent to that of Virginia.

Florida's official race laws stipulated that any mixed-blood person, whether of White/Negro, White/Indian, Indian/Negro, White/Hispanic, or whatever, were to be legally and socially classified as Mulatto.

Before 1850, federal censuses were performed primarily for tax and land ownership recording purposes, and most Indians were either not recorded, or included in the other free persons or free persons of color categories. Beginning in 1850, persons contracted to perform the federal census were encouraged to inquire as to person's self-identification due to the fear of, "Light skinned Negroes trying to pass themselves off as Whites or Indians."

Given that there were only three available categories, White, Black, or Mulatto; that persons who appeared to be obviously mixed-blooded of any kind were to be listed as mulatto; and that persons taxed could not be listed as Indian (who were inherently non-taxed); it is not surprising that there were few persons recorded as Indian east of the Mississippi from 1850 to 1900. For a perfect example of the confusion suffered by lawmakers attempting to place these mixed-bloods into some neat category, read this excerpt from the 1871 North Carolina Joint Senate and House Committee as they interviewed Robeson County Judge Giles Leitch about the free persons of color living within his county:

Senate: Half of the colored population?

Leitch: Yes Sir; half of the colored population of Robeson County were never slaves at all...

Senate: What are they; are they Negroes?

Leitch: Well sir, I desire to tell you the truth as near as I can; but I really do not know what they are; I think they are a mixture of Spanish, Portuguese and Indian...

Senate: You think they are mixed Negroes and Indians?

Leitch: I do not think that in that class of population there is much Negro blood at all; of that half of the colored population that I have attempted to describe all have always been free...They are called "mulattoes" that is the name they are known by, as contradistinguished from Negroes...I think they are of Indian origin.

Senate: I understand you to say that these seven or eight hundred persons that you designate as mulattoes are not Negroes but are a mixture of Portuguese and Spanish, white blood and Indian blood, you think they are not generally Negroes?

Leitch: I do not think the Negro blood predominates.

Senate: the word "mulatto" means a cross between the white and the Negro?

Leitch: Yes sir.

Senate: You do not mean the word to be understood in that sense when applied to these people?

Leitch: I really do not know how to describe those people.

Regardless of the tax or land reasoning behind the Mulatto classification, a close examination of other factors can give a clearer picture of a group's social and legal standing. Although members of the Apalachicola River settlements of Cheraw Indians were marked as Mulatto on federal censuses, they were not held to the same legal or social restrictions as free persons of Negro blood. For example, Florida Legislation of 1848 required free Negroes and mulattoes to have a White guardian appointed by the local magistrate and were restricted from owning property. No person in Florida of Catawba origin was ever assigned a White guardian, and Jacob and Absalom Scott were both early Florida landowners. Jacob Scott's 160 acres, mill and ferry were valued at $2,000 in 1860, actually making him one of Calhoun County's more prosperous citizens.

As the country hung on the edge of Civil War, the southern White power structure was making huge efforts to dis-empower and regulate any non-White non-slave persons in their midst. White slave owners feared that free Negroes, Mulattoes and Indians held natural anti-slavery sentiment and would support the North should war break out. To encourage free mixed-bloods to move beyond the boundaries of their states, many southern Legislatures approved tax regulations which imposed double taxes on free persons of color, required them to pay tax on their wives (a financial burden not imposed on White households) and restricted them from carrying firearms.

Every state, which passed these restrictions, was the subject of petitions by Indian individuals and families who felt that they should not be the subjects of such free person of color laws. In 1857, William Chavis was arrested and charged as a free person of color with carrying a shotgun, a violation of North Carolina state law. He was convicted, but promptly appealed, claiming that the law only restricted free Negroes, not persons of color. The appeals Court reversed the lower Court, finding that:

Free persons of color may be, then, for all we can see, persons colored by Indian blood, or persons descended from Negro ancestors beyond the fourth degree.[1]

Prior to 1850, the Catawba who had settled on the Apalachicola were recorded as other free persons or free persons of color on Jackson and Calhoun County tax rolls. In 1856, Florida tax books changed their format from a free persons of color bracket to a free Negroes and Mulattos bracket. At that point, the Catawba were taxed as White. After the conclusion of the Civil War the tax books changed again, this time with the race of an entire page of taxed persons being listed at the top of the page. On these new books, some of the Catawba head of households are taxed as White, some are taxed as Colored, and the several inter-related Scott families were listed on a separate page with no racial header. Often the tax records of Jackson and Calhoun disagree with the racial classification of Cheraw-Catawba recorded on the federal census. Taxed as free persons of color Jacob Scott and his wife Polly Harmon are recorded as White on the 1850 census, and then later as Mulatto on the 1860. Francis E. Hill and his wife Elizabeth Scott are first censused as White in 1850, then as Mulatto in 1860, while Francis Hill was consistently taxed as White.

As has been discussed by many scholars, the Indian stereotype was already prevalent among eastern Whites as early as the 1850's. The typical understanding among southern Whites was that all Indians had long hair, did not speak English, and, most importantly, all lived out west. Eastern Indian descendants were known to have varying hair colors and textures, varying eye colors, and a wide

---

[1] See *State v. William Chavers*, 1857 North Carolina, Frank W Sweet, *Legal History of the Color Line* (Palm Coast: Backintyme, 2005) 182.

range of skin complexions, even as early as the 1700's, most probably due to intermarriage with early Spanish, French, and English traders. Most officials were at a loss when trying to categorize these people into a social structure that allowed for only two races, Black and White. An excerpt from the 1910 petition of the Croatan Indians of Sampson County, North Carolina, shows the prevalent attitude of southern Whites towards mixed-blood Indians:

> Since 1868, the white people in Sampson County, as a rule, have classed these Indians with the Negroes and refused to accept them except as Negroes. They have consequently been forced, in a measure, with the Negro race, but they steadfastly refused to be classed with Negroes. They have refused to attend the churches and the schools of the Negroes or to co-mingle with them on terms of social equality. It is marvelous that they have been able to maintain their racial status so well under the adverse social and political status which has been forced upon them by the white people.

Physically described over the years as dark skin-dark hair-dark eyes, mixed-blooded almost White, at the least mixed-blooded, Caucasian-Indian and to quote the Jackson County School Superintendent:

> From their appearance can very easily be considered as belonging to the white race...of course possible that they might have a large percentage of Indian blood.

We must take all of the evidence as a whole, boil it down, and come to a conclusion. The Apalachicola River Cheraw were considered to be persons of Indian ancestry, and were not legally or socially held to the restrictions of bearing Negro blood.

Green Corn Dance
Blountstown Ceremonial Grounds, 1995

3. "A Company of Friendly Indians" The Florida Frontier

The previous two chapters discussed the overall state of the remnant eastern-Siouan/Cheraw people in the late 1700's to early 1800's, and the racial climate they had to endure daily. In turning our attention to the history of the immigrant Cheraw-Catawba Indian community of northwest Florida, we must address their ancestral families, and their tribal origins. Most of the family groups who migrated into Florida in the 1820's, had previously maintained residence on the dwindling Catawba reservation lands in northwestern South Carolina. By the time of the Florida migration, most of the reservation lands had been leased to White farmers, and the Catawba were surviving economically by the collection of lease payments and pottery sales. The lack of land to live on, and the inability of the government of South Carolina to collect the White settlers' lease payments, caused many Catawba families to migrate outside the Carolinas, many going south, others to the west. The core of the Catawba families who settled into Florida bore the surnames of the major early Catawba families, Ayers, Brown, Scott and Stephens. Jacob Scott,

Joseph Scott, and Absalom Scott were direct familial connections to the Catawba reservation, and Isham Scott (possibly a cousin to the former three) had connections to the Catawba-Siouan Indians on the Gingaskin land in Northampton, Virginia. Richard Jeffries, also a core member of the Florida Catawba, was the son of Silvia Scott and Andrew 'Drury' Jeffries (grandfather of Parker Jeffries mentioned later) who also had ties to the Catawba in Northampton. Jeffreys/Jeffries descendants have been identified as descendant of the Catawba tribe in many different places, and in different eras. By 1842 several members of the Jeffries family had migrated to Greene County, Ohio, where Parker Jeffries filed a Supreme Court case after he was denied the right to vote. The jury found:

> That the plaintiff is of the Indian race, the illegitimate son of a white man and a woman of the Indian race, and that he has not more than one fourth of the Indian race in his veins.

R.F. Dill, a Greene County, Ohio historian, published in 1881 a compilation of short biographies of leading Greene County residents. Here he mentioned:

> James Jeffreys...son of Silas and Susan Jeffreys...Silas was a descendant of the Catawba Tribe of Indians. ...
> Mason Jeffreys...son of Uriah and Caroline Jeffreys...Uriah was a descendant of the Tribe of Catawba Indians.

Over ten years later, and hundreds of miles to the south, another document of Jeffreys Catawba descendancy arises. In 1881 Dr Joseph McDowell, of Fairmont, Georgia filed a petition with the U.S. Senate and the Indian Office asking for, "Catawba Indians, and 81 in number" The report stated that "William Guy, of Granville, GA (sic NC), and Simon Jeffries, of Bellville, VA, Catawba Indians, served five years in the Army (Rev War) and were honorably discharged, and these people are their descendants."

That Catawba families had migrated into northwest Florida is beyond doubt. In September, 1853, a band of 18 Indians, all of whom claimed to be Catawba, was reported by Brigadier General G.B. Hall as wandering near Stockton, Alabama (near present-day Atmore, Alabama). Their leader was named Taylor, and the band represented two families: Taylor and Houser. There were four men in the group; the rest were women and children. They said they came from northwest Florida, and were en route to Arkansas, but were stranded for lack of money and had been begging corn and potatoes in Alabama where residents were anxious to get rid of them. The fate of the Houser family remains unknown, but the Taylor family established a household among the Creeks in Atmore, Alabama.

When the Catawba families arrived, they were not the only Indians in the area; however, plans were already underway to clean the landscape of the Creek and Seminoles residing there. By the end of 1839 the final emigration of the Creek Indians living within the treaty reserves along the Apalachicola was complete, except for several bands of hostiles still hiding in swamps, and several communities of White Stick Friendly Creek allowed to stay according to the stipulations of the Treaty of Fort Jackson. However, treaty, tax, and census documents record the presence of another group of Indians living in the area of the Apalachicola River. These 'other' Indians were obviously considered different and separate from the Creeks. After leasing out all their land on the reservation, and possibly hoping to continue a tradition of military honor, a handful of Catawba families ventured into northwest Florida. After serving as friendly Indian scouts against the hostile Creeks and Seminoles, these mixed-blood Indian families settled down into quiet lives as farmers, stock keepers, and ferry operators, just as they had previously done in South Carolina.

The presence of Catawba Indian families in the Apalachicola River valley can be documented as far back as 1828, when Absalom Scott, Jacob Scott and his wife Polly Harmon, Richard Jeffers, John Jones, and Joseph Scott appear on Jackson County tax records. It does not appear that any Catawba were present prior to that time, as they are not mentioned in the Treaty of Moultrie Creek of 1823. It appears that even service as scouts in the militia would not guarantee complete safety; however, and in 1837 the families of Betsy Ayers and Sally Ayers were mistaken for hostile Indians and held at Dog Island by Lt. Berrian in preparation for removal to Indian Territory. The family members of Betsy and Sally were eventually adopted into citizenship in the Choctaw Nation along with several other Catawba families.

1833 Tax Book of Jackson County Florida those taxed as free persons of color		
Beady	taxed $3.00	owned no land
Betsy	taxed $3.00	owned no land
Ireland, Samuel	taxed $3.00	owned no land
Jones, John	taxed $3.00	owned no land
Scott, Jacob	taxed $3.00	80 acres
Scott, Absalom	taxed $3.00	20 acres
Scott, Olive	taxed $3.00	owned no land
Scott, Penny	taxed $3.00	owned no land
Scott, Luranny	taxed $3.00	owned no land
Ward, Terressa	taxed $3.00	owned no land

1834 Tax Book of Jackson County Florida those taxed as free persons of color	
Brooks, Martin	taxed $.25
Jeffers, Richard	taxed $.25
Jones, John	taxed $.25
Maseleno, Joe	taxed $,25
Scott, Jacob	taxed $.25
Scott, Absalom	taxed $.25
Scott, Joseph	taxed $.25

In the September 1823 treaty of Moultrie Creek, a special provision was added by the Chiefs present which read:

> One mile square, at the Ocheesee Bluffs, embracing Stephen Richards' fields of said bluff, be conveyed, in simple, to said Stephen Richards.

Richards, of North Carolina, was homesteading in Calhoun County prior to 1820, and was serving as an interpreter for U.S. Indian Agent Gad Humphreys. Richards continued his work as interpreter in the May 1832 treaty of Payne's Landing. On October 15, 1837, Captain Stephen Richards was empowered by the West Florida Militia to form and outfit a mounted company of Indians for service against hostile Creeks and Seminoles. Most of the recruits for this Company were Creek Indians from the newly created Apalachicola reservations, yet there are many persons appearing on the Company roll that bore English names and were from such areas as North Carolina and Virginia.

Captain Stephen Richards' Company of Friendly Indians
Mounted Florida Militia
Enlisted 1837 at Walker's Town, Jackson County, Florida

Amotto	Jake
Tom Fobby	Ponna
Madison	Towny
Sledge	Johny Chopka
J.H. Bison	Jimmy
Fo-load-ree	James Richards Sr.
Moses Manning	Charles Walker
Sumpkai	Cosi-es-a-hola
Black Billy	Spanish John
Friday	James Richards Jr.
John Mealey	Jim Walker
Tailor	Davy
Black John	Josee
Anthony Garshaw	John Richards
John Newcommer	John Walker
Te-pikie	Big Davy
Bob	Peter Leonard
William Gay	John G. Richards
Nit-ti-e	Wilsie
Tomma	U-lousa or Davy
Samuel Bray	Lewy (killed 16 Apr. 1838)
J.D. Gill	Stephen Richards
No-co-ceola	Jackson Wood
Old Tommy	Eat-cot-to
William Brown	Loceo-tie
William Goodrum	W. Riley
Oak-kos-kee	Silas Wood
To- or Captain Billy	R.B. Evans
Martin Caseboury	Chebon Louc
Hawkins	Samsey
George Perryman	Isaac Yellowhair
Colonel Toney	James E. Fairley
Gilbert Chermichael	Samse Succo
Heischa	James Sessions
Thomas Perryman	Mr. Fobby
To-tour or Capt. Billy	Chebon Lusta
Davy Chopka	William Simmon(s)

The names of William Brown, R.B. Evans, James E. Farley, and John Newcommer are particularly interesting. Later censuses would later identify these individuals as being born in either South Carolina or Virginia, and James Farley was identified as Indian after he later moved to Georgia. A Captain Newcomer signed a 1753 letter along with the famous Catawba King Hagler, and Indian Trader John Evans was mentioned as having a "half-breed son among the Catawba Nation" in 1733.

When the Creek Indians agreed to emigrate in 1838 and 1839, Captain Stephen Richards lost the majority of his Indian recruits. Nevertheless, it is apparent that there were Indians still residing in the area that Richards could rely on for support. A military report from 1844 (5 years after the last band of Creeks had immigrated to Indian Territory) reveals that, not only were roving groups of hostile Creeks still a real threat, but that there still remained in the area a group of Indians from whom Richards could recruit.

> Captain Stephen Richards and a company of friendly Indians dispatched to search for renegade Indians that attacked passengers of Henry A. Nunes' barge at Phillips' Inlet.

The Catawba were willing to shed the blood of their own race to protect their White benefactors. Nevertheless, this did not guarantee their own protection, even from those whom they had tried to protect.

Joseph Scott had been living in the area of Calhoun County since at least 1834, when he first appears on tax books as a free male of color. The household of Joe Scott was the only home headed by a free person of color documented on the 1840 census of Calhoun County where he was listed as between 51 and 60 years of age. It appears that Joe was a respected and well-known leader of his people then, but still even that position and title was not enough to save his life. In 1846, Old Chief Joe, a well-known Indian Chief, was stabbed in the head by a White man in an altercation over a roll of calico cloth. Chief Joe's son (probably the younger Joe Scott who appears on the 1850 census) was present and witnessed his father fall. According to the 1846 newspaper account, Old Chief Joe called out to his son Thwatka which is most certainly a variant or mispronunciation of the Siouan phrase *Thwalka*, which translates to "he has killed me."

The area where Old Chief Joe was killed appears on an 1842 map of northwest Florida as Dead Lakes. The name of this area of lakes and swamps is undoubtedly a reference to the numerous dead cypress trees that naturally fill the lakes and streams of this area. Cheraw families continued to live in this area, which is contiguous to the Scotts Ferry settlement.

The violent death of the beloved Chief Joe obviously sent ripples of fear through the local Catawba families and they seem to have temporarily abandoned their habits of wandering the area hunting and fishing. On the 1850 Federal census, the Catawba are recorded as living in a tightly grouped settlement on the Ocheesee district (north-west area of Calhoun County) property of their White benefactor, Captain Richards. This fear was not long standing however, and the Catawba gradually returned to their custom of having hunting and fishing camps. The families of Thomas Ayers, Susan Smith, James Martin and Malachi Scott are recorded as doing just that on the 1880 census of southern Calhoun County. As stated earlier, the 1850 Federal census shows the Ayers, Brown, Scott, Quinn, Stephens, and Hill Catawba families settled on the Richards' property at the Ocheesee Bluffs near the Apalachicola River.

This was also near the Gregory House and Hotel, a popular stopping point at Ocheesee Landing for river traffic. In 1848 (nine years after the Creeks had emigrated) a

Frenchman visiting the Gregory House sketched and painted a group of Indians and Native structures he titled "Indian Village on the Apalachicola."

Indian Village on the Apalachicola

1850 Federal Census of Calhoun County - 5th Division						
household name		age	sex	race	occupation	born in
56 Ayers	Ishmael	46	m			SC
"	Abigail	50	f			SC
"	James	22	m			GA
"	Thomas	14	m			SC
"	John	13	m			GA
"	Solomon	11	m			GA
"	Ishmael	8	m			GA
57 Hall	David S.	23	m			ALA
"	Rebeck	22	f			GA
"	Susan	7	f			ALA
"	Amlin	6	m			ALA

"	Thomas	1	m			FL
58 Scott	Joseph	38	m	M		GA
"	Mary	35	f	M		GA
Gray	Michal	34	m			Ireland
59 Quinn	Joseph	30	m	M		SC
Jones	Eliza	28	f	M		GA
"	Susan	5	f	M		FL
"	Delila	1	f	M		FL
60 Stafford	Joseph	33	m			VA
"	Mary	22	f			ALA
61 Stafford	William	53	m			GA
62 Scott	Mary	30	f	M		GA
"	John	20	m	M		FL
63 Scott	Jacob	53	m		Smith	SC
"	Appa	45	f			SC
"	James	16	m			GA
"	Nancy	14	f			GA
"	Luzinia	12	f			GA
"	Lewis W.	10	m			GA
"	Jacob	9	m			ALA
"	Henrietta	8	f			ALA
"	Susanna	7	f			ALA
"	Lewisain	6	f			ALA
"	Malvin	1	m			FL
64 Scott	Isham	69	m	M		NC
	Millia	46	f	M		SC
65 Loftis	Paskel	45	m			Tenn
Jones	Olive	46	f	M		GA

"	Lark	24	m	M	FL
"	Elizar Ann	5	f	M	FL
"	Thomas	2	m	M	FL
66 Scott	Abslom	60	m	M	NC
"	Gillatia	38	f		NC
"	Jacob	17	m	M	FL
"	Amanda	14	f	M	FL
"	Mary Ann	11	f	M	GA
"	John T.	9	m	M	GA
"	Samuel	5	m	M	FL
"	Henry	2	m	M	FL
Stevens	Alexander	20	m	M	FL
67 Butts	James	26	m		ALA
Jones	Mary Ann	20	f	M	GA
68 Hill	Francis A.	38	m		ALA
"	Dicy	28	f		SC
"	Marthey	6	f		GA
"	Ann	2	f		FL
69 Scott	Jacob	38	m	M	GA
"	Lewrania	76	f	M	NC
"	John M.	16	m	M	FL
70 Castleberry	Sarah Ann	23	f		GA
Brown	Emaline	7	f		FL
Castleberry	Lewranny	11/12	f		FL

Just across the Apalachicola River, in then far southern Gadsden County, another portion of the Catawba had settled temporarily on the Forbes Purchase lands. Documented on this census was a repeat of William Stafford's household—Henry Mainer, Tom Scott who had married Sarah Larkins, Frances Larkins, and William (Billie) Scott.

1850 Federal Census of Gadsden County – Southern District						
household name		age	sex	race	occupation	born in
618 Stafford	William	58	m		farmer	SC
"	Mary	52	f			SC
"	Frances	26	f			SC
"	William	20	m		overseer	FL
"	John	14	m			FL
"	Ann	10	f			FL
619 Maner	Henry	28	m		farmer	SC
"	Sarah	27	f			SC
"	Martin	3	m			Texas
620 Scott	Thomas	22	m		farmer	SC
"	Sarah	17	f			FL
621 Larkins	Frances	38	f			NC
"	William	19	m		farmer	SC
622 Scott	William	24	m		farmer	SC
"	Martha	17	f			SC
"	John	15	m			SC
"	Henry	9/12	m			FL

An interesting event occurred just seven years after the recording of this census. In 1857 James Butts (head of household number 67) was called before the Jackson County Court to answer to charges of adultery and fornication with a free Mulatto. Butts challenged the charge based on the fact that the female he had been co-habitating with did not fit the legal definition of a Mulatto. Several White witnesses were called including Captain Stephen Richards and John Chason, and the Judge dismissed the charge.

The awarding of military service land grants in the mid 1850's resulted in a split of the original Ocheesee Bluffs Catawba settlement. Jacob Scott chose 160 acres at the site where old Joe Scott had lived in southern Calhoun

County on the Chipola River. Here Jacob constructed a ferry service and mill. This settlement became known as Scott's Ferry, as it is still known today.

Absalom Scott lived briefly at Scott's Ferry until a close friend, John Chason, acting as Absalom's land agent, was able to secure him an 80-acre tract in southwestern Jackson County at the headwaters of the Chipola. The Ayers family chose land in mid-western Calhoun County near the banks of the Chipola at a site near present-day Clarksville. Having less Indian blood than the other immigrant Catawba families, the Ayers' did not maintain an identifiable separate community and continued to out-marry with local White families. Although they did not continue to be identified as part of the Cheraw-Catawba community, the more socially adept members of the Ayers family did speak out for them on several occasions, and many of the Ayers descendants still speak with pride about their Indian ancestors.

Indoor Stomp Dance, Blountstown Florida 2004

4. "All of whom claim to be Catawbas" The Florida Catawba

General Jacob Scott became 'Chief' of the Catawba in South Carolina after the death of General New River in 1801. General Jacob Scott died in 1821 and General Jacob Ayers succeeded him until his own death on 14 July 1837. Ian Watson in his compilation entitled "Catawba Indian Genealogy" described the death of General Ayers in 1837 as "the end of a conservative era of Catawba tribal government." And indeed, 3 years later the Catawba relinquished their lands in South Carolina and scattered.

The reality of this shift to a more progressive thinking leadership and the eventual self-termination of their reservation status and migration to North Carolina in 1840 may have an ethnic root instead of being the result of acculturation. Watson, Brown and McDowell clearly identify three of the Catawba surnames as being of Cheraw origin (George, Robbins, Harris)[1] and these families seemed to begin a push to dominate the Catawba leadership after the death of General Scott in 1821.

---

[1] Watson, 83; Brown 1966, 218, 249; McDowell 1955, 145).

The exodus of so many Catawba in the 1820's could possibly represent a reaction to the overtaking of the political structure by the mixed-blood Christianized Cheraw. The fact that a large number of Catawba left the reservation in the time-span 1790 to 1830 cannot be doubted. Revolutionary enlistments and petitions of Catawba showed the surnames Williams, Connar (or Conyer), Thompson, Simmons, Jones, Taylor, Cross, Cook, Bullen (or Bowlin), Kennedy, Kelley, Young and Dickson;[2] surnames which do not appear after the 1820's. The Scott family, described by Brown as "a large and prominent family" among the Catawba, supplied three men to the Revolutionary effort, Capt. Jacob Scott, Capt. John Scott, and Billey Scott. If these 3 males were the only Catawba males bearing the 'Scott' surname, then by population estimates the Scott family Catawba must have represented at least 3 households and 15 to 20 individuals, yet by 1849 only two Scott individuals remained connected to the Catawba (John Scott born 1826, and Sam Scott born 1799).[3] By 1853, John Scott was the only individual with that surname associated with the tribe, and the 1943 Catawba Tribal roll does not bear any Catawba with the Scott surname.[4]

So here is the million-dollar question: where did these Catawba go? In 1828 a group of mixed-blood Indians arrived in the area west of the Apalachicola River in northwest Florida. Of the nine surnames present in that

---

[2] Thomas Drennan's company of Catawba Indians paylist of 1780; Petition of "the Chief and head men of Cataba Nation..." 24 Nov 1792, South Carolina Petitions, 1792, #26, South Carolina Department of Archives and History.

[3] Massey, B.S. account of Catawba Indians 1849.

[4] Massey, B.S. Report to the Governor of South Carolina on the Catawba Indians, 1854; "Catawba Tribal Roll, 1 July 1943," #11273-1959-077, part 1, Central Classified Files, Records of the Bureau of Indian Affairs, National Archives, Washington, D.C.

original migration (Ayers, Brown, Bunch, Harmon, Jeffries, Jones, Scott, Stephens, Williams),[5] a whopping seven surnames have been identified as Catawba.[6] The ages of the eldest males in the Florida migration (Jacob Scott born 1797, Isham Scott born 1791, Absalom Scott born 1790)[7] matches the age group of the last remaining Scott elder attached to the Catawba in 1849 (Sam Scott born 1799). Given that the names Sam, George, Tom, John, and Jacob, which appeared with uncommon frequency among the Catawba, also appear with the same frequency among the Florida mixed-bloods; we must accept as fact that the Sam Scott at Catawba and Jacob, Isham and Absalom in Florida were related, most likely brothers and sons of the older Jacob Scott.

That Catawba migrated as far as Florida is without question. As mentioned on page 29, in Sept. 1853, a band of eighteen Indians, all of whom claimed to be Catawba, was reported wandering near Stockton, Alabama. Their leader was named Taylor, and the band represented two families: Taylor and Houser. There were four men in the group; the rest were women and children. They said they came from West Florida and were enroute to Arkansas, but

---

[5] Tax records of Jackson and Calhoun Counties, 1828, 1830, 1831, 1832, 1834, 1835, those individuals identified as "free persons of color" and "other free persons."

[6] Surnames Ayers, Brown, Scott, Stephens, and Williams identified on Rev. War. paylists and reservation land leases. Surname Bunch identified from reservation land leases. Surname Jeffries identified prior to 1900 as Catawba descendants from records of Jenffries/Jeffreys family members residing in Ohio.

[7] 1850 census of Calhoun County, Ocheesee District, plantation of Capt. Stephen Richards.

were stranded for lack of money.[8] The Taylor family eventually settled among the mixed-blood Creeks living on land near Stockton, but the Houser family disappeared from official view.

It is amazing that the family of Richard Taylor appears in the mid-1800's, all claiming to be Catawba Indians, as there had been no records of the Catawba Taylor family since the 1740's when War Captain Tom Taylor was among them.[9] Documents such as this of the Taylor family and also the Jeffries/Jeffreys and Guy families are indicative that Catawba descended families migrated to many areas of the southeast with very little documentation, but have been discounted by academics because they did not bear such well-known Catawba surnames as Harris, Brown, Cantey, etc.

Surname recognition alone is not the only evidence that the Apalachicola mixed-bloods carried a Catawba identity. Their own words support this fact. On July 10th, 1861, Francis Hill, a White unmarried male, was charged by the Calhoun County Court with "Fornication with one Eliza Scott a Mulatto woman." This charge was not long-standing, however, as Francis petitioned and provided witnesses who were prepared to testify that:

> Eliza Scott is not a Mulatto as named in the indictment but is an Indian of the Catawba tribe, her grandfather Jacob Scott being a headman of that tribe.[10]

---

[8] Hall, General G.B. to Capt. I.C. Casey about certain Indians in his County, 12 Nov 1853, Records of the Bureau of Indian Affairs, National Archives, Letters Received, Miscellaneous, 1853, A-172.

[9] Douglas S. Brown, *The Catawba Indians* (Columbia SC: University of South Carolina, 1966), 220, 225-27.

[10] 10 July 1861, State of Florida V. Francis Hill, 1860-65 Calhoun Judicial Cases, Calhoun County Courthouse Archives Room 3rd Floor, Blountstown, Florida.

The testimony seemed sufficient to clear away the cloud of suspicion of negro ancestry, as seems apparent when Francis Hill, Isham Scott, and John 'Capt. Jack' Ayers were all allowed to enlist for Confederate service with McCallister's Calhoun Rangers later in December. As almost an afterthought, the Fall Court filed away the fornication charge with a 'not guilty' finding.

The Ayers Family

During the French and Indian War, the Catawba Indians in South Carolina began adopting the English Military titles of General, Colonel, Captain, etc to describe their tribal leaders and social ranks within the tribe. Many Catawba were already adopting English alongside their Catawba names. Some of these military titles became proper names eventually, for some individuals.

In records of the French and Indian War was the name of Colonel Ayers. He is recorded as the leader of a group of 27 Catawba warriors on an expedition against Fort Duquesne. Ayers became Chief of the Catawba after the death of King Hagler in 1763. In 1764 Chief General Ayers secured a treaty for the Catawba people that allotted them reservation lands totaling 144,000 acres in present day counties of Lancaster, York, and Chester, South Carolina.

In the 1750's there were recorded a total of six Catawba towns, including Newtown, Peedee, Carrow (or Saraw) Sugar Town, Nuestee, and Nawsaw. Catawba Indian agent Hutchison wrote in 1782:

> A number of Indians had it in view to go and live
> among the Cherokee, who had offered them land, and
> proposed to aid them in building houses, but the aged
> among them were averse to removal... At the time I am
> speaking of these men (General Scott, General Ayers,

and General Harris) were old, and would not consent to remove.

The enlistment records of Captain Thomas Drennan's Unit of Catawba Indians in the Revolutionary War, 1783 shows:

-William (Billy) Williams	-Jacob Scott
-Billy Scott	-John Eayrs (Ayers)
-James Eayrs (Ayers)	-Jacob Eayrs (Ayers)
-Little Stephens	

The Revolutionary War Catawba Indian service list (no officer voucher) in 1784 shows:

-Jacob Scott	-Jacob Eayers
-John Scott	-Little Stephens
-William (Billy) Williams	-Billy Scott
-Mosy Ayres	-Colonel John Eayres
-William Billy Eayres	

In 1826, the Catawba Nation occupied only two villages, Newtown on the York County side of the Catawba River, and Turkey Head on the Lancaster side. On June 16, 1826, General Jacob Ayres, Chief of the Catawba's (he succeeded General Jacob Scott as such) signed a lease for 208 acres of the Catawba Reservation lands lying north of the Old Trading Road. Those who signed the writ, in addition to the General, were Colonel Lewis Canty, Captain John Ayres, Major Thomas Brown, and Lieutenant Jessie Ayres.

In 1837, Catawba Chief General William Harris signed a lease for some of the last remaining Catawba Reservation lands over to a White settler. The headmen who co-signed for this lease were Major Sam Scott, Captain Edward Ayers, and lieutenant Lewis Stevens.

Incidentally, Captain John Ayers had already moved to north Florida at this time, there being little room left on the Catawba reservation. He served under Stephens Richards as a friendly Indian from 1837 to 1845, scouting against hostile Creek and Seminole Indians resisting the federal government's efforts to resettle them west of the Mississippi River in the Indian Territory.

On March 13 of 1840, at Nations Ford on the Catawba River, the Leaders of the Catawba signed a treaty that ceded their South Carolina reservation lands that remained in exchange for money to buy lands in Haywood County, North Carolina, among the Cherokee. This treaty was signed by James Kegg, John Joe, Philip Kegg, Allen Harris, David Harris, William George, and Samuel Scott. Captain John Ayers was not a party to this treaty as he was serving with Stephen Richards in Florida against the Seminoles.

Soon after the treaty was signed, the Catawba began moving to the lands they were trying to purchase in North Carolina, but on arriving they found that North Carolina refused their purchase of land. Finding themselves in a difficult situation, they began to contemplate removing to the Indian Territory west of the Mississippi. Throughout the many years since contact with the colonists, and then the Americans, individual Catawbas and small groups had been leaving the reservation for the west, and south, seeking opportunity in other areas.

In February of 1847, after receiving news that the Chickasaw Nation would accept them, thirty Catawba sent a petition to the Commissioner on Indian Affairs entitled "A Petition of Catawba Indians of North Carolina Desiring Assistance to Remove to the West." Signatories to this petition were:

-John Scott	-Rosa Ayres
-Lewis Stevens	-Samuel Scott
-Thomas Stevens	-Mary Ayres
-Margaret Ayres	-Sally Ayres
-Julia Ann Ayres	

On October 4 of 1848, the landless North Carolina Catawbas wrote a letter, this time to President James Polk, requesting formal assistance in removing to Indian Territory with the Chickasaw. Signing this letter to the president were:

-Lewis Stevens	-John Scott
-Thomas Stevens	-Jimmy Ayres
-Mary Ayres	-Margaret Ayres
-Betsy Ayres	-Esther Scott
-Rosa Ayres	-Harriet Stevens

Receiving no financial assistance from this endeavor, they returned to South Carolina and purchased 800 acres in their original county, Some of those who had left did not return to South Carolina though. In 1872, a congressman from Georgia petitioned the Indian Office for assistance in removing 84 Catawba residing in Granvilee County, Georgia. In 1853 a band of 18 Catawba were reported wandering near Stockton Alabama, having traveled there from north Florida. Some Catawba actually made it to Indian Territory, because in 1853, thirteen Catawba were adopted into citizenship by the Choctaw National Council. The Catawba adopted were:

-Betsy Ayers	-Julian Ayers
-Mary Ayers	-Saphronia Ayers
-Sally Ayers	

When the Civil War erupted many Catawba fought for the confederacy. Enlisting in the 17th South Carolina Infantry Regiment were the following Catawba men:

-Jefferson F Ayers	-John Scott
- William Canty	-Alexander Timms

The name of John Ayrs appears on the 1830 census of Greenville District, South Carolina. In 1849 the Catawba Roll lists the following Catawba residing in Greenville district:

Males:
-Franklin Canty age 23   -John Scott age 23
-John Brown age 12   -David Harris age 40
-Billy Brown age 20
2 male children under age 10
Females:
-Polly Ayers age 35   -Betsy Mush age 18
-Elizabeth Canty age 23   -Patsy George age 30
-Jane Ayers age 18   -Esther Brown age 28
-Jinny Joe age 43   -Polly Redhead age 40
-Mary George age 18   -Betsy Hart age 26
-Peggy Canty age 20
6 female children under age 10

In 1854 the Catawba Roll shows:

-Jefferson Ayers age 14   -John Scott age 28
-Polly Ayers age 40

Among the records relating to Catawba families who migrated to Florida and became part of the Cheraw Indians of North Florida Tribe is a grave marker at Whitfield Cemetery that reads, "Captain John Ayers…born 1791… Seminole Wars."

No members of the Ayers family appear on Jackson County tax records prior to 1838, as they were still in the Catawba Nation. In 1840 on page 190 of the Jackson County census the name of William Aires appears.

The names of John Ayrs (age 59…Blacksmith…born 1791 in South Carolina) and his wife Arilla (age 34…born 1816 in Georgia) appear on the 1850 census of Ocheesee District in Calhoun County Florida. Next to them are William (Billy) Williams, Ishmael Ayres, Joseph Scott, Mary Scott, Jacob Scott, Absolom Scott, Alexander Stephens (married to Mary Ann Scott), and Franise (Frank) Hill (Married to Elizabeth Scott). These two being the same couple prosecuted in 1862 in Calhoun County court. Frank Hill would be charged with fornication with a Mulatto. The case was dismissed once it was found that Elizabeth Scott was not a Mulatto under the meaning of Mulatto in the law of the time (being one quarter or more Negro).

The name Aurelia (Arilla) Ayers (age 44...born 1816 in Georgia) appears on page 111 of the Ocheesee district, Calhoun County Florida census alongside James Stephens, Alitha (Ayers) Cutts, and William Ayers (born 1819 in South Carolina). Arilla Ayers's oldest child, John Ayers Jr. is listed as born in Florida in 1838. Members of the Scott and Hill families, as well as Ishmael Ayers, appear in Calhoun County at Scotts Ferry (a bit further down the Apalachicola River valley on a small feeder waterway called the Chipola River near the junction of the two waterways) by 1860.

Florida Civil War Confederate Service Records of the Ayers family:

Ayers, John-born 1839 Florida; married Seania Burnam on 9-11-1862;died 12-16-1862 in Liberty County; enlisted in the 4th Infantry on 5-10-1861 in Jackson County; absent on furlough since 2-27-1862

Ayers, Asa-born 1-9-1846 in Calhoun County; married Sarah Francis Richards on 8-19-1886; died 2-6-1906. Claimed to have served in the 10th Infantry Company F, but not found on rolls of unit (so far)

Ayers, David S.- born 1840 Florida; served in Calhoun Rangers prior to enlisting in the 5th Florida Infantry Company H in 1862 at Rico's Bluff. Mortally wounded 7-2-1863 at Gettysburg.

Ayers, John W. Jr.- born 1837 in Florida; served in Calhoun Rangers prior enlisting in the 5th Florida Infantry Company H in 1862 at Rico's Bluff. Wounded in the foot in June 1864, deserted to the Union forces in November 1864. His father was John Ayers Sr. a descendent stated that John Ayers Sr. died at Rock Bluff, Florida in Liberty County, Florida. He was known as Captain John and served in the Seminole War as a scout.

Ayers, Solomon- born in Florida in 1840; served in the Calhoun Rangers prior to enlisting in the 5th Florida Infantry Company H in 1862 at Rico's Bluff. Died of typhoid 2-9-1863 at Florida Hospital.

Ayers, Thomas- born 1840 in Blountstown in Calhoun County; married Emily Marshall on 3-31-1889; served in Calhoun Rangers prior to enlisting in the 5th Florida Infantry Company H in 1862 at Rico's Bluff. He was captured 4-6-1865 at Farmville Virginia and released on Oath of Loyalty 6-24-1865 at Newport News, Virginia. Described as 5 ft., 10 in. with grey eyes, fair skin, and light hair.

Essie Hill Syfrett, Matriarch,
Blountstown Indian Community

5. "A Motley Crew of Half-Breed Indians" The Civil War

The beginning of the Civil War marked a turbulent time for the Cheraw-Catawba Indians in the Apalachicola River Valley. Obviously influenced by their ancestral warrior culture, they were little concerned with the political or racial aspects of the conflict. Though no immediate negative effects were apparent as the war raged, the after-effects would prove to be near disastrous. Some Catawba enlisting with the Confederate military did not return in as good shape as when they had left, and some did not return at all. The most devastating effects of the war were the legal and social problems the Catawba would face after they had abandoned the doomed Confederate cause.

Under the charismatic influence of John (Captain Jack) Ayers and Indian countryman John Chason, in December of 1861 Isham Scott and Francis (Frank) Hill enlisted with Captain McCallister's Calhoun Rangers. This home guard company served no longer than three months, however many of the soldiers re-enlisted in other Confederate units. In September of 1862, Ruben G. Blanchard (who had married Jane Scott Stone, the granddaughter of

Olive Jones) enlisted with the Confederate Army in Company E, 10th Florida Infantry. Blanchard was soon reassigned to the Confederate Navy in 1864 and served on the ironclad gunboat Palmetto State. Ruben served on the gunboat until Charleston was evacuated, then was re-assigned to the Army. After being captured on April 6, 1865 during General Lee's retreat from Richmond, Blanchard was held in prison at Point Lookout prison in Maryland for two months and released. Despite his unquestionable loyal service to the Confederacy, Ruben was initially denied a Florida Confederate Pension in 1908. This was due, in no small part, to the Chairman of the Calhoun County Commission, George L. Hansford. Hansford refused to approve the pension application of Blanchard, and took the further step to write personal letters to the pension board to accuse Blanchard of being "mixed blooded" and of having joined the Union Blockade Fleet.

Hansford's brother, John D. Hansford, had earlier married Ruben Blanchard's daughter, Mary Jane, and this obviously insulted the racial purity ideals held by George. Though it was clearly documented that Blanchard had served in the Confederate military, the pension board declined to approve Blanchard's pension stating, "Negroes were not enlisted and are not entitled to pensions."

It was only after Blanchard attained the services of Jackson County law firm Calhoun and Campbell, that he was approved for the meager pension. A support letter written by W.M. Ayers stated that Ayers had known Blanchard for over 45 years, and that they had served together during the late War. Blanchard's attorneys chalked the whole affair between Hansford and Blanchard up to, "some would-be officer of Calhoun County who got a little mad with him about his politics."

On September 27 of 1864, Union Cavalry clashed with Confederates at Marianna, Florida. The battle would produce two significant events involving the Apalachicola Catawba.

First, in the heat of battle, John Chason, benefactor of the Catawba and land agent for Absolom Scott, was seriously wounded and captured by Union soldiers. Chason was sent to Ship Island prison where he died of dysentery on December 19 of 1864. The support of the Florida Catawba towards the Confederate cause was destined to die with Chason.

The second interesting occurrence during the battle was a report of Union soldiers capturing a Confederate soldier on horseback, which they first assumed was a Colored man. The soldiers solved this mystery after the capture when they determined that Henry Stevens, the Colored man in question, was of Indian blood.

Confederate enlistment records of Catawba in Florida are a wealth of personal information on the origins and physical descriptions of these early community members:

> Private James G. Stephens enlisted in the 2nd Florida Battalion Company E where he is described as born 1840, living in Marianna, captured in 1864 near Petersburg and released from Elmira Prison in 1865. He was 5 foot 4 inches, hazel eyes, dark skin, dark hair.

> Private Isham Scott enlisted in the Calhoun Home guards where he is described as 5 foot 5 inches, brown eyes, dark hair and dark skin.

> Private John Levy Emanuel enlisted in the 6th Florida Infantry Company D where he is described as born 1843, captured near Nashville in 1864 and sent to Camp Douglas Prison. Mustered into the 5th U.S. Volunteer Infantry in 1865.

> Private Asa Emanuel enlisted in the 6th Florida Infantry Company D where he is described as born 1815 in Georgia, attempted to enlist in 1862 at Apalachicola but was rejected by the inspecting officer. He was a mem-

ber of Watson's Company of Florida Militia and was captured 1864 in Volusia County. He was 5 foot 8 inches, grey hair, grey eyes, dark skin and last appears on a roll at Hilton Head Prison in 1865.

Private Daniel Bunch enlisted in the 6th Florida Infantry Company D where he is described as born 1833, absent on every roll after April 1862 and AWOL since 1863.

Private William Perkins enlisted in the 6th Florida Infantry Company D where he is described as born 1845 in Bibb County, Georgia, discharged 1863 in Mossy Creek Tennessee. He was 5 foot 4 inches, dark skin, dark hair, black eyes.

Private John W. Hill enlisted in the 8th Florida Infantry Company E where he is described as born 1834 in Robeson County, North Carolina. He died of pneumonia in 1862 at Camp Winder Hospital, Richmond, Virginia.

After 1864 it appears that some Florida Catawba abandoned the Confederate cause. Many Catawba who had been serving the Confederacy switched sides and enlisted with the Union. As with the CSA enlistments, the Union service records also contain worthy information about these warriors:

- **Private John T. Scott** enlisted with the 2nd Florida Cavalry Company A where he is described as born 1843 in Early County, Georgia. He was **5 foot 11 inches, black eyes, black hair, dark skin**. He did not return from the War.

- **Private Alexander H. Stephens** enlisted with the 2nd Florida Cavalry Company A where he is described as born 1829 in Jackson County. He was **5 foot 10 inches, dark brown eyes, dark hair, dark skin**. He died of disease during the War and did not return.

- **Private William Bunch** enlisted in the 2nd Florida Cavalry Company A where he is described as born 1845 in Henry County, Alabama. He was **5 foot 6 inches, hazel eyes, dark brown hair, dark skin.**

- **Private Francis M. Williams** enlisted in the 2nd Florida Cavalry Company A where he is described as born 1842 in Calhoun County. He was **5 foot 9 inches, hazel eyes, dark brown hair, dark skin.**

- **Private John Williams** enlisted in the 2nd Florida Cavalry Company A where he is described as born 1845 in Calhoun County. He was **5 foot 8 inches, black eyes, black hair, dark skin.**

- **Private John M. Scott** enlisted in the Florida Ranger Regiment Company A where he is described as "**born in Jackson County in the State of Florida, aged 21 years and by occupation a farmer. This soldier has black eyes, black hair, dark complexion, he is 5 feet 7 ½ inches tall.**"

- **Private Samuel Scott** enlisted in the Florida Ranger Regiment Company A where he is described as "**born in Calhoun County in the State of Florida, aged 19 years and by occupation a farmer. This soldier has black eyes, dark hair, dark complexion, he is 5 feet 8 ½ inches tall.**"

During the final days of the War, Private Wade Richardson wrote of the Union's Florida Cavalry soldiers:

> As to the rank and file they were a motley crew of as dare-devil fellows as can be collected at any seaport town, I guess. Among them were Spaniards, French creoles, half-breed Indians, Germans, a few Poles and a host of crackers and gophers - the western Floridians were derisively called gophers.[1]

---

[1] Wade H. Richardson, "How I Reached the Union Lines," *Milwaukee Telegraph*, 1896.

6. "A Settlement or Town of their Own" Scott's Ferry

After 1850 at least six of the original fifteen Catawba households had resettled at the newly acquired land of Jacob Scott. Jacob owned and operated a ferry service and mill (just as the Catawba had done on the Catawba River), and became quite prosperous, even in comparison to his White neighbors. The movement of the Catawba into southern Calhoun can be tracked by the written history of the local Stone family. In the book *History of Jackson County* it is recounted that:

> Lackland M. Stone, whose father was Colonel Henry D. Stone, one of Jackson County's first settlers, was also an Indian trader. His family settled on the upper Chipola, near the future town of Webbville. When the Indians were moved to Ocheesee, he followed them, as he did later to Iola.

The Stone family had apparently continued to carry a family legacy of Indian trading, because as early as 1691 the Council of Colonial Virginia had recorded:

Thomas Blunt is appointed interpreter to the Indians on the south side of the James River, David Whitley to the Indians at the head of Rapp'a River, and William Stone to the Indians on the head of Yorke River.

And also in 1778, The North Carolina General Assembly enacted that,

Be it enacted, that Willaim Williams, Thomas Pugh, Willie Jones, Simon Turner, and Zedekiah Stone, be, and they are hereby appointed commissioners for said Indians.

The reference to the Indians being moved to Ocheesee, does not describe any documented Creek band, as they had never maintained a village on the Chipola, did not have a village at Ocheesee, and had emigrated to Texas or Indian Territory before the Stone family moved to southern Calhoun at Iola. Bird Attaway (first husband of Elizabeth Perkins) and Horace Ely were contracted by the Jackson County Commission to build the first bridge across the Chipola at a location described as "near Webbville." Combine all of the above with the fact that the 1840 census of Calhoun County records Joe Scott as having a family of 17 free Colored persons living next to John Chason and Henry D. Stone at Iola, and there can be no doubt as to this identification of the Cheraw-Catawba identity of the settlement.

The Scott's Ferry settlement was located at Range 9 west, 2 south, section 21, adjoining the Chipola River. This was the route used to travel from any spot in eastern Jackson or Calhoun Counties along the Apalachicola over land to Port Saint Joe. The Scott's Ferry settlement appears on the 1860 census as a clearly defined separate community, and the families living there were recorded on a special census page, though the racial identification of them was confused and clearly tainted by racial prejudice. The 1860 federal census was performed during the height of the racial tensions between the pro-slavery South and the abolitionist North. Families who had previously been identified as "free persons of Color–non Negro" or Mulatto were suddenly reclassified as free Negro on this census, though they were still White or "free persons of color" on local tax records. In 1848, legislation was passed in Florida which required free Negroes to have White guardians appointed by the local Courts. No Catawba was assigned a guardian. Free Negroes and mulattoes could not legally own land. Jacob Scott and Absalom Scott held clear title to their land. In 1861, legislation passed which required free Blacks to register with a probate judge or be classified as a slave and claimed by a White person. It is clear that none of these laws were ever applied to the Apalachicola Catawba.

At that time, only Whites were allowed to testify or serve as jurors in court cases involving Whites. And yet, an 1840 prospective jury list included Robert and Joseph Blanchard (originally of Gates County, North Carolina), Joseph Montford, Jonathan Jones, and Robert Scott. John Chason and Jaspers Scott were called as witnesses in the Jackson County Court case, *State V. James Butts* in 1857 (Butts had been living with Mary Ann Jones since at least 1850). And Martha Hill Minton was reimbursed for traveling 24 miles in 1863 in order to testify for Sherrod Scott. Samuel Scott was even an eligible voter in Jackson County in 1869.

In 1860, the census reflects the Scott's Ferry settlement as consisting of six households. Living there at that time was Jacob Scott and his nephew Joe, living in one household along with Joe's wife Sarah Brown Castelberry, and Sarah's daughter Emiline Brown. Francis (Frank) Hill and his wife Elizabeth Perkins Attaway held one home, and William Stafford and his wife Polly Harmon Scott (former wife of Jacob Scott) held another. Jack Howard inhabited a household along with Lofty Bunch as his wife, along with his two sister-in-laws Betty Bunch and Molly Thompson (who later married Shurard Scott).

Paschal Loftis and Olive Jones shared a home along with her granddaughter, Jane Scott. The last remaining household was that of Isham Scott and his wife Jane Manuel who shared their home with her father, Edmund Manuel (originally of Sampson County, North Carolina and a veteran of the Sampson County Regiment 4th Company in 1812).

1860 CENSUS OF CALHOUN COUNTY....SCOTT'S FERRY...SPECIAL CENSUS PAGE				
HOUSE #	NAME:	AGE:	RACE:	BORN IN:
165	SCOTT, Joe	43	MU	ALA
	" " , Sarah	36	MU	FL
	" " , William	8	MU	FL
	" " , Polly	6	MU	FL
	" " , Ellen	4	MU	FL
	" " , Jack	8/12	MU	FL
	" " , Jacob	60	MU	ALA
	BROWN, Emiline	16	W	FL
166	HILL, Frank	43	MU	ALA
	" " , Eliza	35	MU	FL
	" " , Delila	16	MU	FL
	" " , Ann	10	MU	FL
	" " , Joe	8	MU	FL
	" " , Quinn	7	MU	FL
	" " , Bob	6	MU	FL
	" " , Blunt	4	MU	FL
	" " , Green	1	MU	FL
167	STAFFORD, William	65	W	NC
	" " , Polly	55	MU	ALA
	" " , Jim	16	MU	FL
168	HOWARD, Jack	26	MU	FL
	" " , Lofty	20	W	ALA
	BUNCH, Betty	23	W	ALA
	THOMPSON, Molly	22	W	GA

169	LOFTIS, Paschal	60	MU	NC
	" ", Olive	50	MU	ALA
	SCOTT, Jane	20	MU	FL
170	SCOTT, Isham	65	MU	ALA
	" ", Jane	45	MU	ALA
	MANUEL, Edmund	67	MU	ALA

At the bottom of this special census page, John G. Smith, the census taker, added his personal opinion of the racial make-up of this settlement. Either Smith had never personally traveled to the settlement and gathered his information from other citizens (as was sometimes the case when census takers were trying to list far-out settlements), or Smith was given misleading information by the settlement citizens themselves, because almost all of the information other than the actual names of the community members was wrong. The age and birthplace of almost every community member does not compare to that listed for the 1850 or 1870 census. The only justice performed by Smith with this document is held in the second sentence of his commentary where he bears witness that these Indians lived in a settlement separate from White or Black persons:

> The Free Negroes in this county are mixed blooded almost white and have intermarried with a low class of whites – Have no trade, occupation or profession they live in a settlement or Town of their own their personal property consists of Cattle and Hogs, They make no produce except corn and peas and very little of that, They are a lazy Indolant and worthless race.

Back on the Catawba reservation, the annual report of Catawba Agent J.R. Patton to the South Carolina Senate uses, strangely almost exactly, the same wording to describe the Indians still residing there:

> They are a somewhat indolent and careless people living in small Log Houses or cabins covered with boards and are not settled together in a Town or village but

> scattered over a considerable portion of the land they
> occupy they own but little furniture of any value a por-
> tion of them work small farms or patches of corn but as
> a general thing do not make anything like a support
> they own some Horses a few Cattle and some Hogs.
> This seems to sum up the amount of what They possess.

Oral history of the Apalachicola Cheraw-Catawba reflects that Eliza Scott Hill had been educated as a child in
South Carolina, taught basic education to all the children of
the Scott's ferry community, and also traveled briefly back
to the reservation to teach school but was not well received, and soon returned to Florida. The 1861 Annual Report of Catawba Agent J.R. Patton seems to verify this oral
history as it reflects that Eliza Scott (Indian) was paid $20
for teaching during that year.

Elsewhere in the southeast, Indian communities were
being described in almost exactly the same words. In 1840,
36 White residents of Robeson County, North Carolina appealed to the Legislative Assembly to regulate the sale of
spirits to the Lumbee Indians (who are also of Cheraw ancestry):

> The County of Robeson is cursed with a free-coloured
> population that migrated originally from the districts
> round the Roanoke and Neuse Rivers. They are gener-
> ally indolent, roguish, improvident, and dissipated.
> Having no regard for character, they are under no re-
> straint but what the law imposes.

The fact that Smith classified the Catawba in Florida
as free Negroes with no trade or occupation, and in general
being lazy and worthless, betrays his racist views. He could
not have been completely blind to the fact that these people
operated a mill and ferry, because even Smith took note
that the colony's total worth was over $4,000 (which in
1860 made it one of the wealthiest small towns in Calhoun
County).

Scott's Ferry's founder, Jacob Scott, passed away by 1862 and Joseph Scott held the property title. Penny Scott was taxed for 200 acres she supposedly owned across the river in what would become Liberty County. In 1858, Joseph Scott was assessed for taxes at $100 for real estate, $525 for cattle, and $30 for household furnishings. When the War closed in 1865, the Indians paid dearly for their change of sides. The local Whites apparently decided that the County Court would be the vehicle they would use to facilitate their harassment. In the fall term of 1862, Francis Hill was brought up on charges of fornication with a Mulatto, but was found not guilty. In 1866 a series of charges were pressed against the Catawba, beginning with Gilberry Scott being charged with open state of fornication and Sabra J. Register with attempting to marry a mulatto. John M. Scott, a Union veteran, was also charged with open state of fornication in the fall term. All of these charges were discharged with "not guilty" verdicts at the close of the fall term in 1866. Due either to the crisis level post-War economy or to legal harassment, it is clear that the Scott's Ferry Town had begun a downward spiral. By 1870 the total households had increased to nine, but the total worth of the settlement had decreased to $1,440.

1870 CENSUS OF CALHOUN COUNTY – PAGE # 20					
HOUSE #	NAME:	AGE:	RACE:	OCCUPATION:	BORN IN:
256	BLANCHARD, Ruben	28	M	Farmer	ALA
	" ", Eliza	23	M		FL
	" ", John	2	M		FL
257	empty				
258	JONES, Olive	65	M	Keeping house	GA
	" ", Martha	?	M		GA
259	EMANUEL, Edmond	70	M	At home	NC
260	WILLIAMS, Thomas W.	45	M	Farmer	FL
		24	M	Keeping house	ALA

	STEVENS, Susan				
		77	M	Farmer	NC
261	SCOTT, Isham	34	M	Keeping house	GA
	" " , Jane				
		36	M	Home keeper	GA
262	SCOTT, Polly	14	M	At home	ALA
	MUMFORD, Nancy				
263	Empty				
		62	M	Farmer	GA
264	JONES, John	26	M	Keeping house	FL
	" " , Beady	7	M		FL
	" " , William	6	M		FL
	" " , Jack	3	M		FL
	" " , Emily	1	M		FL
	" " , Martha				
265	WILLIAMS, Jane	48	M	Keeping house	GA
	" " , Delia	22	M	At home	FL
	" " , William	20	M	At home	FL

By the time of the 1880 census, Scott's Ferry appeared to be making a comeback. The settlement now contained eleven households and the compact town seemed to suffer some drift, as a few families were listed as living a few miles up the Chipola River in the Abe's Springs area. This small splinter settlement contained five households beginning with the home of Henry Johnson who had W.D. Williams living there as a boarder. Penny Scott maintained a household as well as William Scott. Nancy Montford was keeping her own house now, and the final home was Enoch Wells. A significant clue as to the temporary split off of these families could be the fact that those at Abe's Springs listed their occupation as logging.

Back at the original settlement, we find eleven homes starting with Benjamin Beauchamp and his wife Ellen Scott who had his stepdaughter, Sallie Washington living as his servant, and Richard Nixon as an orphan. George Green had settled here with his wife Dora Butts. Elizabeth Scott Hill shared a home with her stepdaughter, Nancy Quinn, her son Joseph Quinn, and her son Frank Hill. William Quinn and his wife, Rena were living here, as well as

Henry Johnson (this is a repeat of the Henry Johnson household from Abe's Springs). John (Jack) Jones and his wife Beady Mainer were still here in 1880 living next to Mary Scott, who was sharing a home with her daughter-in-law, Julian Scott and her grandson, William Scott. New resident Sam Washington held a home next to Olive Scott Jones who shared her home with her daughter, Martha Jones, a servant named Mary Linton, a boarder named T.C. Shelby, and another servant named Hester Brouchard. Ruben Blanchard and his wife Jane Stone were still living at Scott's Ferry at this time, and the final home was held by David Martin (originally from Person County, North Carolina) along with his wife Amanda Scott. Living with David Martin was a servant, Polly Gibson, and David's daughter Mary (who would later marry Barney Locklear).

Nearly 40 years later the name of T.C.Shelby would be brought up again in reference to Scott's Ferry, but this time in his home state of Kentucky. An excerpt of the 1918 Kentucky case of McGoodwin v. Shelby, ruled over by Judge Sampson of the Marion Circuit Court, stated that:

> In May, 1915, Miss Florrie Hood, a most eccentric and peculiar woman, died intestate, childless,and unmarried, at her home in Lebanon, Kentucky, she being about seventy years of age, and the owner by inheritance of several houses and lots and some acreage property in the city of Lebanon, and quite an amount of personal property...There were no close relatives living so far as known, however, that one Thomas C. Shelby, a nephew of Miss Hood, had many years before left Marion County on account of trouble and had gone to Florida.

After dispatching investigators throughout Florida and mailing 1,500 postcards to different post offices in search of Thomas Shelby or his descendants, the estate administrators located Shelby's widow and two minor children—sole heirs to the Hood fortune. The problem was that Shelby's widow:

> Was the daughter of William Scott, and William Scott was the son of Joe Scott, and Joe Scott was supposed to be a mulatto, so that the mother of the children of Thomas C. Shelby was not a pure-blooded white woman.

This would make the parents' marriage illegal and render the children bastards incapable of inheriting. Instead of trying to prove that the family of Shelby's widow did, or did not, have negro blood, the parties reached an out-of-court settlement to distribute the property among themselves. The case then wound its way through the Kentucky court system for the next three years. First, the original probate court disallowed the agreement as:

> Being unconscionable since the children could not be considered anything but White, their forefathers having not associated with negroes, but with Whites.

In the end, the Kentucky Court of Appeals ruled that regardless of the ancestry of the children, all witnesses agreed they could not possibly bear enough negro blood to be considered mulatto as described by Kentucky law.[1]

By 1885 the timber industry had taken root along the Apalachicola and Chipola Rivers, and had assisted the Scott's Ferry settlement to swell to seventeen households. Eight persons listed their occupation as logman, seven as farmer, and three as laborer. The drift present in 1880 is not noticed in 1885, and most of the families had returned to the original settlement site. The town still consisted of Scott, Quinn, Williams, Hill, Green, Johnson, and Martin households, but also now held the homes of Edmon Davis, Henry Mainer, and William Perkins (son of Elizabeth Per-

---

[1] See *McGoodwin v. Shelby*, 1918 Kentucky, Frank W Sweet, *Legal History of the Color Line* (Palm Coast: Backintyme, 2005) 449-51.

kins and half-brother of Mary Attaway Scott) who had been living in Jackson County. Some surviving court records from this time provide an excellent example of the depth of interrelation and cooperation that existed in the settlement at this time. When Louvinia Martin Brown (wife of Tom) was charged in 1904 with assault with intent to murder and carrying Winchester rifle without permit, her defense witnesses included Thomas Ash, Dave Martin and Linnie Davis. Henry Atkins was charged with murder in 1907 and Wesley Williams, M. Mainer, Tom Scott and Jeff Scott were called as witnesses to the event. Reuben Blanchard, Bill Jones, Mary Blanchard, and Rosa Quinn were brought to court to answer charges of larceny of a bateau.

After the death of Martha Jones, Thomas Butts was appointed administrator of her estate and most of her property was distributed between John Howard, Rueben G. Blanchard, and George Green. When John Howard was appointed guardian of Margaret Bunch in 1890, John Williams was appointed as surety. Thomas M. Scott was left parentless in 1893, George Green was appointed guardian of the 15 year-old boy, and Francis M. Williams and Joseph Quinn were sureties. In 1894 Beady Mainer Jones approached the Court to administer the estate of her deceased husband, Jack Jones. William Quinn was listed as her surety while J.W. Blanchard was appointed by the Court to appraise Jack Jones' personal property. When David Martin was appointed legal guardian of his half-brother's and sisters (after the death of his mother, Annie Scott Hunter), Sandy Davis was listed as surety. After 1910, some Indians began to make claims for pensions based on their Confederate service.

Letters from other settlement members supported almost all of the Cheraw-Catawba in Calhoun County who filed their claims. Rueben G. Blanchard enlisted the support of W.M. Ayers, Elizabeth McDaniel Jones had help from Lawrence and Sarah Williams, and Charles E. Scott received support from Nathaniel Scott, J.M. Atkins, and Cornelius Stephens. The 1917 Civilian Draft Registrations provide as much, if not more, valuable information as the earlier Civil War records. At least nine individuals within Calhoun County were listed as White-Indian citizens. These included members of the Whitfield family (descendants of George Whitfield who married a Scott woman), Herbert Boone (son of Henry Boone and Anna Scott), Lemuel Moses, and John Moses (relatives of Elizabeth Moses Conyers). Another individual, Willie Porter (son of Mathias Porter of Scott Town), was recorded as being Indian Creole and described as having blue eyes and light colored hair. General Quinn of Scott's Ferry was listed as self-employed in farming, having a dependent mother, and also as having blue eyes and light colored hair. No race was listed for Quinn, but his death certificate issued in Bay County stated that the mortician considered him White.

The year 1917 also marked a series of yearly floods on the Chipola and Apalachicola Rivers, which caused the abandonment of the original settlement site. Later census records show that community members had established home sites due northwest of the Scott's Ferry site, at an area now known as Marysville. Land titles to the original settlement were maintained, however, as was the old cemetery. In October of 1920, Samuel F. Scott and Elizabeth Scott were both recorded as "C.I." in the race category on the Shiloh District voter's registry book for Calhoun County. This is the same Samuel and Elizabeth Scott who appear on the 1920 census of Shiloh Precinct, Marysville to Scott's Ferry Road. Samuel Frank Scott was the son of Samuel Scott and Jane Ayers of Scott Town settlement in Jackson County. Samuel Scott senior was the son of Absolom Scott and Gilly Stephens, the founders of Scott

Town. In 1929, Samuel F. Scott was appointed as executor of the estate of his cousin, John Williams, in Calhoun County. Many groups of Creek Indian descendants from Georgia and the Florida panhandle tried to use these records in their petitions for acknowledgement by the federal government to show continuation of a Creek presence in the area, but as we have shown these persons were clearly of Carolina Cheraw origins, not Creek.

Education for their children would also force the Catawba out of their self-imposed isolation, and provide for the only documents pertaining to them during this time period. In 1938 David Martin, trustee for the Marysville school, had a letter written to Calhoun County Clerk of Court J.A. Peacock which stated:

> There are men who would knife us out of having our own school, saying that we are negroe. You know our character that we are of white and Indian blood.

In reference to a 1944 investigation by the Jackson County School Board, the Board members made inquiry regarding "Sweetie Blanchard from Scott's Ferry," whose sons were the students whose ancestry had been called into question by the authorities. The Board members solved the dispute by suggesting that the two Johnson boys should attend school in Calhoun County.

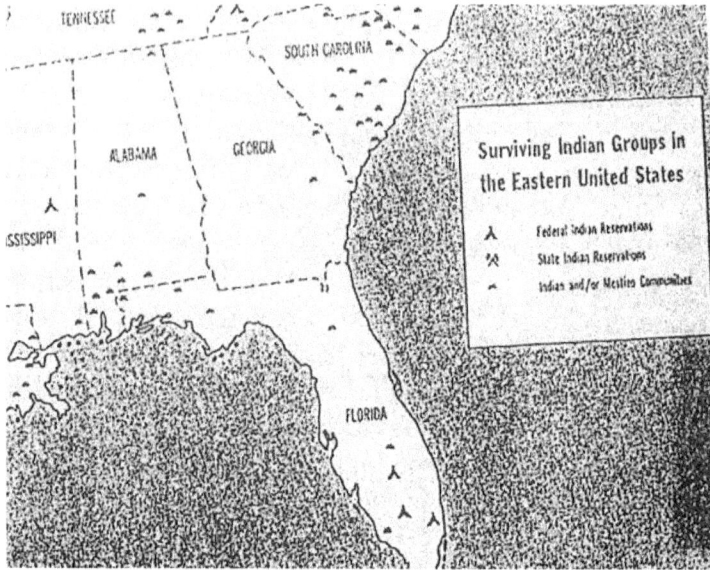

Surviving Indian Groups in the Eastern United States

In the 1948 annual report of the Smithsonian Institution, William Harlen Gilbert Jr. published a compilation entitled "Surviving Indian Groups of the Eastern United States." Though Gilbert never visited north Florida himself, he did visit the so-called Creeks at Atmore, Alabama (whose Hathcock, Gibson, Allen, and Taylor ancestors were Cheraw). It is apparent that during one of these trips to Alabama Gilbert gathered second-hand information regarding a group of mixed-blooded Indian persons in Calhoun (Daisy Porter Nichols was living in Flomaton near the Creek reservation at that time, and may have been the source of this information). In the last paragraph of the Florida section of Gilbert's report he states:

> Aside from the Seminoles there are other small mixed groups of possible Indian descent in Florida. Around Pensacola are to be found the Creole mixed people of Escambia County and in the same area are certain groups of Creeks from across the border in Alabama.

Some 100 miles to the east near Blountstown in Calhoun County there is said to be a colony of Melungeons from Tennessee.

The "Melungeons from Tennessee" of whom Gilbert speaks are an ethnic group of mixed-blood persons in the area of eastern Tennessee whose main family surnames were Gibson, Collins, Goins, and Bunch. These persons also descended from Siouan Indian ancestors who had spread westward from the Virginia/North Carolina border. Since none of the Apalachicola River area Cheraw-Catawba reported Tennessee as their birthplace, and they were not locally known as Melungeon, Gilbert either relied on a second hand opinion, or maybe even made his own personal judgment based on the Bunch and Goins ancestors of some of the Florida Catawba.

Gilbert did do justice, however, by identifying the fact that the Apalachicola River Cheraw-Catawba lived in a colony, separate from their White and Black neighbors, well into the mid-twentieth Century. The identification of a separate Indian community in the area of Calhoun and Jackson County of northwest Florida was repeated by Brewton Berry in his book *Almost White* published in 1963.

Mathias Porter and his wife Ella Goodson
Jackson County Florida

This is some information on the Porter family, a core
family of The Cheraw Indians of North Florida, from the
book on Lumbees correlated with the Jane Blanks Barnwell's 2007 edition on Lumbee cemeteries entitled Sacred
Grounds.

PORTER The grantor and grantee index for Robeson,
1787-1939, shows Samuel Porter with twelve tracts on
drounding [sic] Creek, Raft Swamp and Ashpole

Swamp between 1788 and 1799, John Porter with two deeds 1802-1808, north of Ten Mile, Britton, 1809, Etheldred, 1833, Spencer and Catherine, 1838, and Richard 1841. Porter was listed as an Indian name in Howellsville Township in 1870 census of Robeson. Listed in the 1900 Indian census schedule of Robeson County, Porter was listed as full blood from Florida, and as Indian in the 1930 census of Pembroke Township. Death records show the Indian name Porter in 1922 in Alfordsville and Saddletree townships. They were related to the Dial, Hardin, Hunt, and Lowery families. Name cited at the Locklear/Porter family cemetery at Prospect UM Church by Jane Blanks Barn-hill, Sacred Grounds, 2007, a listing of 162 Lumbee cemeteries in Robeson County.

Poarch Creek Families of Cheraw Ancestry

During the resurgence of the Creek identity in the southeast that intensified with the Creek Indian Land Claims cases in the 1950's and peaked in the 1980's, there were many thousands of people doing genealogical work on hundreds of ancestral family lines, many in hopes of finding Creek ancestors and being part of the settlement. For others it was due to actual interest in their own Indian heritage. As a part of the process leading to the federal acknowledgement of the Poarch Band of Creeks, there was a substantial amount of research conducted by various academics as well as countless lay researchers. The Bureau of Acknowledgement and Research within the B.I.A. also delved into the area. In the course of this researching into the roots of the Poarch Creek community, many ancestors of Poarch Creek Indians were found to have Carolina Cheraw Indian origins. As Poarch Creek Indian researchers, Lou Vickery and Steve Travis state in their book released in 2009 entitled, *Rise of the Poarch Band of Creek Indians*:

> It is noteworthy that the Sizemores, Gibsons, Hollingers, Durant, and Marlows, were all mixed-blood lines that came to southwest Alabama from South Carolina. Most were mixed-bloods from the Catawba or Lumbee tribes.[2]

> The McGhee and Rolin families, along with the Moniacs, Gibsons, and Ehlerts, were the genetic founders of the contemporary Poarch Band of Creek Indians.[3]

> Along with the Dees family, the Hathcocks migrated from South Carolina to the Poarch area where they intermarried with the Poarch Creeks.[4]

> The Hathcocks were originally not Creek Indians. Like the Dees and Gibson familes, the Hathcocks came from the South Carolina area, they were a mixture of Portuguese and Native American, who intermarried with Lumbee Indians.[5]

> William David Bart Gibson was born about 1823 in South Carolina, arriving in Alabama in the early 1840's.[6]

> Listed as a half Creek Indian, (Arthur) Sizemore probably had some Catawba/Lumbee bloodlines.[7]

---

[2] Lou Vickery and Steve Travis, *Rise of the Poarch Band of Creek Indians* (2009), 144.

[3] Ibid., 147.

[4] Ibid., 154.

[5] Ibid., 161.

[6] Ibid., 154.

[7] Ibid., 155.

Cheraw Indians of North Florida on the 1840, 1850, 1860, 1870 Census from the Scott Town and Scott's Ferry Community Census Records

Below are some references to various census documents that record shifts in the populations of the two core communities at Scott Town and Scotts Ferry over the decades since their arrival in Florida.

Arrived in late 1828....Joe Scott appears on 1840 census of Calhoun County as free colored persons (5 males 12 females) in Iola (present day Scott's Ferry area) living next to John Chason and Indian trader Henry D. Stone....a few households over were Jackson J. Wood and Moses Manning (who appeared on Richards' Co. of Friendly Indians--most likely had Cheraw wives).

1850 Calhoun County Census – the name John Williams (this should be household #52) (note: John Williams was born 1790 in Mecklenburg NC where he appears in 1820 and 1830 then moved to Robeson Co. where he appears in 1840, then on to Florida by 1850). This entry begins a three-page section which was the core of the Cheraw Indian community living on the plantation of Capt. Stephen Richards. Entries include Ishmael Ayers, Jacob Scott and his wife Appa (Polly) Harmon, Isham Scott, Olive Jones, Absalom Scott, Alexander Stephens, Elizabeth Perkins Hill, and Sarah Brown Castleberry. Another entry is James Butts, who was brought up to court in Jackson County for "Adultery and fornication with free Mulattoe" in 1857, but case was dropped by the state after hearing testimony from John Chason. Also in this county, see household #50 John Williams. The last household of interest is #88 headed by Abigail Brickhouse. Her daughter, Elizabeth Brickhouse, married Ellis F. Davis (of Scott Church).

Also in this household is Sarah (Sabrey) J. Register who married John M. Scott. Just across the river in Liberty County, observe household #618 William Stafford, #619 Henry Maner (sic Mainer ..note that his son was born 1847 in Texas) #620 Thomas Scott (and wife Sarah Larkins) #621 Frances Larkins and #622 William Scott.

Incidentally, the names of Jacob Scott, Joseph Scott, and William Scott all appear on an 1825 petition, in the authors' possession, of Catawba Indians regarding leases of Catawba Reservation land.

1850 Jackson County Census – observe household #522 Samuel H. Ireland (married Elizabeth Perkins, possibly believe first cousin of Betty Perkins, in Gates Co. NC). Next is #523 Betsy Hills (this is a repeat of Calhoun household #68), and #524 Polly Bedie

1860 Calhoun County Census – observe special census page beginning with household #165 Joe Scott (his wife Sarah Beasley-a descendant of the Chowan Beasley family from Gates County NC). This entry marks the begining of the Scott's Ferry settlement including Jacob Scott, Frank Hill, his wife Elizabeth Perkins, William Stafford, Jack Howard, his wife Lofty Bunch, Pachal Loftis, and his wife Olive Jones. Living with Loftis was Olive's grandaughter, Jane Scott, who married Rueben Blanchard. The census also lists Isham Scott, his wife Jane Emanuel and Edmund Manuel (sic. Edmund Emanuel was from Sampson Co. NC and had enlisted there in the War of 1812).

1860 Jackson County Census – observe two pages begining with household #106. Ellis Davis (his wife Elizabeth Brickhouse), #107 Absalom Scott, #108 John Williams, #109 Daniel Bunch, #139 Emiline Davis, #140 Joseph Davis and his wife Susan Emanuel, #141 Joseph D. Smith, #142 Samuel Ireland and his wife Elila Perkins, #143 Alexander Stephens and his wife Mary Matilda Scott.

Incidentally, Alexander died of disease during the Civil War and Mary Matilda remarried to James William Perkins, the son of Elizabeth Perkins Attaway. This was the beginning of the Scott Church settlement.

In 1851, there was a large migration of the Red Bones out of the Rapides Parish area of LA following the "Raw Hyde and Bloody Fight" that took place at Walnut Hill, LA. Many went to east Texas, but the Larimore and Davis families probably came down into Florida at that time.

1870 Calhoun County Census – observe a closely grouped settlement beginning with household #256, Ruben Blanchard and his wife Jane Scott Stone—the granddaughter of Olive Jones—and ending 8 households later with #265 Jane Williams. This was the core of the Scott's Ferry settlement.

1870 Franklin County Census – observe household #21, John Bunch, who was taxed as a free person of Color in Calhoun Co. in 1852, and #22 John Scott, the John M. Scott who married Sabra J. Register. They continued to live in Frankiln County after she was charged with "Attempting to Marry a Mulattoe" in Calhoun Co., most likely due to John's service for the Union in the War. Investigation was held and charges dropped, but they did not live in Calhoun after that.

1870 Jackson County Census – observe a closely grouped settlement beginning with household #37, William Perkins (James William Perkins, living with Mary Matilda Scott, widow of Alexander Stephens). William was charged with "Lewd and Lascivious Cohabitation" in Jackson County Court in 1872 and thereafter moved down to Scott's Ferry). The next entry is #40, Samuel Scott. He was charged with adultery in Jackson County Court in 1868. His first wife, Susan Ireland, filed for divorce that same year. He then remarried to Jane Ayers. Entry #41 is Louis (Lewis) Scott and his wife Isabella Davis).

Further entries are: #42 Henry Scott and his wife Sarah Ayers, #43 Absalom Scott and his second wife Julia A. Bell, #45 Mary L. Chason, daughter of John Chason who had been killed in the War, #46 Abraham Colwell, who was taxed as a free person of Color in Jackson Co. in 1845 and 1846, and again as a free person of Color in Calhoun County in 1852, #47 Wright Colwell, son of Abraham, and his wife Margaret Miller, #48 Pollie Whitehead, #49 Laboring Goodson and his wife Nancy Colwell, daughter of Abraham, #50 Rebecca Duffin (Rebecca Goins, she had two daughters by a white man named 'Duffin'), and #51 Nancy A. Maddox.

Entry #52, Mary Scott, is Mary Attaway. She had married John T. Scott, son of Absalom, but he had died in the War. She had two daughters by him, William Anne and Bell. Then she had an illegitimate son, Mathias, by Jacob Porter. Also living with her here is her mother Elizabeth (Betsy) Perkins. This was the core of the Scott Church settlement.

The Cheraw Indian Research Project was forwarded a very useful document. It is a report by Melinda Maynor on a community of Lumbees who settled in southeast Georgia (Bulloch County) to work in the timber industry.[8] It details the types of work that they performed and its economic impact. It also mentions the period when the industry moved from Georgia to Florida. Its most exciting detail is the mention of Beasley Bullard, a Lumbee born in Robeson, who subsequently lived at Scott Church in 1920, where he is censused as Mulatto. He married Loula Scott

---

[8] Maynor, Melinda M. "People and Place: Croatan Indians in Jim Crow Georgia 1890-1920" Thesis, University of North Carolina at Chapel Hill, 2002 43 pgs.

then moved back to Robeson by 1930, where he is censused as Indian. Apparently Bealsey was living in the
Lumbee community in Bulloch Co. Ga. in 1910, but had
followed the timber industry down to Scott Church and
Scott's Ferry by 1920.

7. "A Large Percentage of Indian Blood" Scott Town

Just after 1860, Absalom Scott, veteran of the Seminole conflicts, acquired the help of John Chason and secured a military service land grant of 80 acres in southwestern Jackson County. Two of Absalom's sons, Lewis and Samuel, would later be granted title to this land, which would become known as Scott Town. Though this settlement started as quite diverse (including the Davis, Williams, Bunch, Jones, Scott and Stephens families), it would eventually narrow to represent only the Scott and Perkins lines.

1860 CENSUS OF JACKSON COUNTY....SCOTT TOWN			
HOUSE # NAME:	AGE:	RACE:	BORN IN:
106 DAVIS, Ellis F.	46	W	Mississippi
" " , Elizabeth (Brickhouse)	32	W	S. Carolina
107 SCOTT, Abb	70	MU	S. Carolina
" " , Gilly (Stephens)	43	MU	S. Carolina
" " , John	17	MU	FL
" " , Samuel	14	MU	FL

	" " , Henry	12	MU	FL
108	WILLIAMS, John	78	MU	N. Carolina
	" " , Vina	37	MU	Georgia
	" " , Simmons	18	MU	FL
	" " , Daniel	16	MU	FL
	" " , John	14	MU	FL
	" " , Benjamin	11	MU	FL
	" " , Henry	?	MU	FL
109	BUNCH, Daniel	24	W	Alabama
	" " , Elizabeth	21	W	FL
	" " , Mary S.	3/12	W	FL
---	---	---	---	---
139	DAVIS, Emiline			
	STONE, Henry S.			
	" " , Mary			
	" " , Emily			
	" " , Georgia			
	DAVIS, Ann E.			
	Unnamed infant			
140	DAVIS, Joseph	43	W	Mississippi
	" " , Susan (Emanuel)	23	W	Georgia
	" " , Frances	15	W	FL
	" " , John	7	W	FL
	DeVAUGHN, Robert	21	W	FL
	ALLISON, William	31	W	FL
141	SMITH, Joseph W.	28	W	FL
	" " , Elmyra J. (Padgett)	26	W	FL
	PEACOCK, Green	17	W	Georgia
142	IRELAND, Samuel	70	MU	Maryland
	" " , Eliza	62	MU	N. Carolina
	" " , Harriett	19	MU	FL

" " , Susan	14	MU	FL
" " , Catherine	11	MU	FL
143 STEPHENS, Alexander	32	MU	FL
" " , Matilda (Scott)	19	MU	FL
" " , Edward	14	MU	FL
ATKINSON, William J.	22	MU	FL
---	---	---	---
155 MAYO, John P.	42	W	Georgia
" " , Nancy	34	W	N. Carolina
" " , James B.	15	W	FL
" " , John H.	13	W	FL
" " , Martha A.	10	W	FL
" " , Nancy F.	8	W	FL
" " , Elijah P.	6	W	FL
" " , Ann M.F.	1	W	FL
MAINER, Milly A.	34	MU	Georgia

In 1860 the Scott Town community consisted of at least 10 households. The main occupation of these families was farming, and that trend has continued to the present day. The first household listed is that of Ellis Davis and his wife Elizabeth Brickhouse. Next door is Absalom Scott and his wife Gilly Stephens. John Williams kept a home with his wife Vina, and so did David Bunch and his wife Elizabeth. John Williams was living in Mecklenburgh, NC in 1820 and 1830, but living in Robeson NC in 1840. Living alone was James Butts Sr., and next door was John Jones Jr., who was to marry Beady Mainer in one year.

Joseph Davis and his wife Susan Emanuel shared their home with Robert DeVaughn and William Allison. Joseph Smith was maintaining a homestead with his wife Elmyra Padgett, and next door was Samuel Ireland and his wife Eliza. Alexander H. Stephens and his wife Mary

Matilda Scott had the last household, which they shared with William J. Adkinson. By the time of the 1870 census, some fairly significant events had taken place at Scott Town. After going A.W.O.L. from Confederate service, Daniel Bunch did not return to Jackson County. Alexander H. Stephens was kept from ever returning by a fatal disease, and in a strange twist of fate, John T. Scott was killed by Confederate fire during his service in the U.S. Cavalry. John would leave behind an Indian bride, Mary Attaway (daughter of Betsy Perkins), who would become a long-lived family leader at Scott Town. After returning from the War, John Williams and John (Jack) Jones had moved down to Scott's Ferry along with their wives and children. Mary Attaway was the daughter of Betsy Perkins, an Indian born between 1822 and 1825 in North Carolina, and Bird B. Attaway, a White riverboat captain working on the Chipola River. Betsy is listed on the 1838 local census of Jackson County as being the head of a household of four free persons of Color.

Scott Town, as it appears on the 1870 census, was composed of seven households, all employed in farming. The first appearing is the home of James William Perkins and his wife Mary Matilda Scott (the widow of Alexander H. Stephens). Living in the Perkins home were Mary's four children by Alexander and her two sons by William. Next was the home of Confederate and Union veteran Samuel Scott along with his wife Jane Ayers. Living next door was Lewis Scott and his wife Elizabeth Isabella Davis, as well as Henry Scott and his wife Sarah Ayers. Still maintaining a household was Absalom Scott along with his new wife Julie A. Bell. The next home was that of Mary L. Chason, orphaned daughter of John Chason. The final household was that of Mary Attaway Scott, the widow of John T. Scott, who shared her home with her mother Betsy Perkins.

1870 CENSUS OF JACKSON COUNTY....SCOTT TOWN			
HOUSE #	NAME:	AGE:	RACE:	BORN IN:
37	PERKINS, William	30	MU	FL
	" ", Matlida (Scott)	29	MU	Georgia
	STEPHENS, Edwin	11	MU	FL
	" ", Gideon E.	9	MU	FL
	" ", George W.	7	MU	FL
	" ", Susan M.	5	MU	FL
	PERKINS, James	4	MU	FL
	" ", John W.	1	MU	FL
40	SCOTT, Samuel	24	MU	FL
	" ", Jane (Ayers)	24	W	Georgia
	BASSETT, John	19	MU	FL
41	SCOTT, Louis	27	B	Alabama
	" ", Isabella (Davis)	30	B	Mississippi
	" ", Vina	5	MU	FL
	" ", Louis	4	MU	FL
42	SCOTT, Henry	22	MU	FL
	" ", Sarah (Ayers)	19	W	Georgia
	" ", Henry A.	4	MU	FL
43	SCOTT, Absalom	78	MU	Georgia
	" ", Julie A. (Bell)	44	W	Alabama
	" ", William S.	4	MU	FL
	" ", James W.	7	MU	FL
45	CHASON, Mary L.	34	W	FL
	" ", Sarah A.	29	W	FL
	" ", Elizabeth	25	W	FL
	" ", Matilda	22	W	FL
----	----	----	----	----
52	SCOTT, Mary (Attaway)	25	MU	FL
	" ", Willie Ann	9	MU	FL

| " " , Bell | 6 | MU | FL |
| PERKINS, Betsy | 40 | MU | N. Carolina |

In 1880 the settlement had continued to decrease, now containing only six homes. Appearing on the census was the household of Lewis Scott and his wife Isabella Davis, while next door was the home of Matilda Davis (sister of Isabella), which she shared with her niece and nephew, Viney Robinson and Washington Boggs. Living alone was John Miller who reported that his father was born in Sweden. Ezekiel Goodson maintained a home which he shared with his Indian wife Rebecca Goins. Living next door was James William Perkins and his wife Matilda Scott Stephens. Henry A. Scott, the son of Henry Scott and Sarah Ayers, had been living with them in 1870, but was now living in the household of his uncle, James Perkins. Still unmarried, Mary Attaway Scott was still keeping her own household along with her daughters William Ann and Rosabella, except that now she also had a son, Mathias, who had been fathered by a local White man of the Porter family.

Very little information is available for the twenty years between 1880 and 1900. The 1885 regular census completely omitted Scott Town, and these individuals were probably recorded on a separate Indian schedule, which has been lost or misplaced. The settlement continued its steady decline and the 1900 census reflects only four homes present. Mary Attaway Scott, now the eldest of the community and a strong family leader, shared her house with eldest daughter William Ann (who never married but had a house full of children). Next door was Mary's younger daughter, Bell Scott, who also never married but shared her home with a boarder, Ed Stephens, the son of Alexander H. Stephens and Matilda Scott. Maude E. Perkins was also maintaining a household as well as Mathias Scott Porter and his wife Louella Goodson (daughter of Rebecca Goins). In October 1903 concerned White Jackson County citizens began a petition which would affect both the Scott Town and Scott's Ferry inhabitants. To quote the book *History of Jackson County* by J. Randall Stanley:

> There were the children of families whose Caucasian purety was questionable. Motives behind petitions to bar children of these families from white schools had to be scrutinized carefully, as it was a problem which might lead to considerable embarrassment, if not actual trouble. In October, 1903, a petition was presented to the Board to bar the children of two families from white schools. The Board entered an order prohibiting them from attending white schools until further notice. The Board stated it was inclined to believe they are entitled to the benefits of the school, they having heretofore attended without complaint and the complaint is not general.

Though the School Board eventually voted to allow the Scott and Perkins children to attend White schools, it was of little importance to them as they had already taken steps to solve the problem. Mary Scott pooled the settlement's resources and had a building constructed for use as a schoolhouse. This one room building eventually was used as both a school and a church. The Scott Church building still stands today, though it is in great disrepair. The involvement of America in World War One caused a new viewpoint to be presented on the racial makeup of the Scott Town people. All of the male children of William Ann and Bell Scott are represented within the civil enlistment records on 1917, and all are recorded as Caucasian-Indian. The five men listed as being of Caucasian and Indian race were Samuel (Sandy) Scott, Thomas F. Scott, Jesse Scott, Jimmie Scott, and George Scott. George was actually inducted into service as a private in the Army and in the race section the inductor crossed through the words *White* and *Colored* and wrote in the word *Indian*. Also inducted into the Army was Sanders S. Scott (sic Samuel) who was listed as White.

The 1920 census showed nine homes at Scott Town, and all apparently on land owned by Mary Attaway Scott. The first of these homes was that of widower Mathias Scott Porter. Living next door was Mathias' son Willie Porter (who had been listed as Indian Creole on WWI civil enlistment for Scott's Ferry). The next household was that of Cromes Rainey, a Negro employee of Mary Scott. William Ann Scott was now head of her own household, which she shared with her children, three grandchildren (Jonas Thomas, Paul Porter and Loula Bell Porter—Paul and Loula attended school at Scott's Ferry) and a lodger, Ed Quinn, formerly of Scott's Ferry. Samuel (Sandy) Scott had the next house, and next door was Kate Scott.

William (Bill) Scott (son of Joe Scott of Scott's Ferry), who had been working at Scott's Ferry since at least 1885, was now back living at Scott Town and sharing a home with the elderly Mary Attaway Scott. The next home was kept by Beasley Bullard, a Lumbee Indian from Robeson County, North Carolina, who along with his wife Loula Scott, shared their home with Earl Batson, a hired hand. Earl Batson would later marry Mary Dasher of Woods. The last household is that of Thomas F. Scott and his wife Daisy Porter. The inhabitants of Scott Town seemed content to live out their quiet farming lives, and under the direction of community leaders such as Mary Scott, William Ann Scott and Tom Scott, they were able to go on farming, turpentining, hunting and fishing with little interference or contact with the outside world.

It was only in 1939, due to the ambition of a bright young girl, that new information surfaced. Mary Francis

Porter was born the daughter of Bessie Porter Copeland in the Scott Town settlement. Bessie was the daughter of Mathias Porter and Louella Goodson (the daughter of Ezekiel Goodson and Rebecca Goins). According to her mother, Mary Francis was the illegitimate child of Whit Wells, a White man. Mary Francis was apparently not satisfied with ending her education at the last grade offered at the little one room Scott School, and she left Florida to receive higher training at the Cherokee Indian Normal School at Pembroke, North Carolina. This school was founded in 1887 as the Croatan Normal School, and in the nineteen teens was changed to the Cherokee Indian Normal School.

It was funded by the state of North Carolina for the education of Indian students of the area. Several other Porter family members were also living in Robeson in 1930 (Dock Porter and his wife Pearly Blanchard; and Coy Porter and his wife Daisy Blanchard, all recorded as Indian on the Robeson County census). Their move may have been inspired by Beasley Bullard and his wife Loula Scott's moving to Robeson in the late 1920's. Apparently not having any knowledge of Indians from Northwest Florida, the school officials requested additional information from the Jackson County School Superintendent. Thus began a series of letters that gives a wealth of information as to the genealogy of the Scott Town mixed-bloods, their racial self-identification, and the attitude of local Whites towards them.

On October 13, 1938, J.R. Lowry, a Lumbee Indian and Dean of the Cherokee Indian Normal School, inquired of the Jackson County post master:

> Is there a school in your town or county by the name of "Scott's School"? [If so], please send me the name of the principal or head of the School. [And tell me] For what race is it maintained? (White or Colored).

The postmaster forwarded the request to C.P. Finlayson, Superintendent of Public Instruction for Jackson County. Finlayson responded to Lowry:

> In the community of the school there are several families of Scotts who from appearance can very easily be considered as belonging to the white race. However, it is generally believed in this county that they have some negro blood in them and for that reason they attend a negro school. It is of course possible that they might have a large percentage of Indian blood but I have no information or knowledge as to their ancestry.

The information regarding negro ancestry inspired Mary's teacher, Mrs. G. Revels, to write a personal letter to Finlayson where she states:

> To write back immediately and answer the questions which I have asked you. It's a shame for Mary to have to miss school when I am certain that she has not a bit of colored blood. She is one of the best students in her class...Please let me hear from you at once regarding this matter.

Indeed, even Mary Francis herself felt it was necessary to write Finlayson to receive fair treatment,

> If you will go out among my people you will find that none of them has had ambition to get out to school for an education and for that simple cause I would like to bring a light to them in that instance...I cannot help the situation among my people and yet I know that a drop of negro blood is not within me.

Finlayson, obviously moved by Mary's letter, started an investigation into the issue. On February 28, 1939, he returned a letter to Mrs. Revels,

> In an effort to learn the true facts I made three visits to the community in which the Scott school is located and

in spite of this effort I am still unable to give you any official statement as to her ancestors.

Finlayson goes on to state that White citizens of the county believed them to have Negro blood, but very little. Finlayson himself was unable to substantiate that claim, and further states,

> The mother and grandfather with whom I talked claim there was no negro blood in their veins but there was Indian blood. This I was of course unable to substantiate by any official records since there seem to be no records.

In this letter Finlayson included two hand drawn family trees outlining the ancestry of Mary Francis Porter that were provided to him by Bessie Copeland and Mathias Porter. According to these notes, Mary Francis was the great-granddaughter of Rebecca Goins Goodson who was half Indian and half White, and the great-granddaughter of Mary Attaway Scott who was also half Indian and half White.

Mary Francis's half-brother, Armond Copeland, also kindled a series of letters when he was employed at the U.S. Naval Ordinance Plant in Macon, Georgia. In March and April of 1945, inquiries were made as to Copeland's ancestry and the Jackson County School Superintendent at the time, J.D. Milton, obviously referred directly to the Mary Francis letters as he replied:

> Some of the forefathers claim there was no negro blood, but there was Indian blood. This, we are unable to substantiate by any official records.

In 1944 another case came before the Jackson County School Board much like the one that had surfaced in 1903. In this case, the School Board would come to a conclusion which had much less backbone. Two Johnson children had been barred from the Grand Ridge School because of questions as to their ancestry. Notes from the Board's investigation reveal that the boys were children of Sweetie Blanchard of Scott's Ferry. The Board interviewed Woodie Staley, a Black man living at Scott Town, and several White citizens.

The Board was trying to determine the eligibility of the boys to attend Grand Ridge School based on whether their relatives attended White or Colored schools in other areas. The Board was at a total loss when it discovered that relatives of the Johnson boys attended school at Marysville/Scott's Ferry, a separate school, and at Woods, also a separate school. Unable to come to any conclusion, Board member Bishop advised them to quit Grand Ridge School due to crowded conditions and attend in Calhoun County.

Jim Scott with the Copeland Girls
Jackson County Florida

The people of Scott Town
Mathias Porter and Tom Scott on the far left

8. "Like Other Good Indians" The Woods Community

Hill, Conyers, Oxendine, Jacobs, Brown

At the beginning of 1900, lumber companies in Georgia faced a dwindling supply of hardwoods, and so turned their attention to northwest Florida. Huge supplies of timber were available and easily accessible for harvesting on both banks of the Apalachicola River. By 1910 such companies as Graves Brothers, Cypress Lumber, Chipola Turpentine, Neal Timber, and Southern Hardwoods were busy installing large timber mills in both Liberty and Calhoun Counties. Many Lumbee Indians of Robeson County, North Carolina, who had left their homeland in the late 1800's for timber employment in Georgia, followed the industry down to Florida. The largest number of Lumbee families, including the Oxendines, Revels', and Jacobs', settled into Liberty County on the eastern side of the Apalachicola, and it is here that they came into close continuous contact with the long-established Florida Cheraw-Catawba families. The combined effort of these two Indian groups to maintain gainful employment in timber resulted in the formation of an Indian settlement in Liberty County known as Woods. This settlement had several Hill families of Creek descent, who had intermarried with the Cheraw. Also living in the community as well were several White families who had lived in the area for generations. Today many descendants of the original Woods settlement still live there as well as in the nearby communities of Bristol and Hosford.

Some descendants of the Woods area Oxendine family today live in Jackson County in the Marianna and Cottondale areas, as well as many descendants of Noah Hill, who was identified as Citizen-Indian on his 1918 military enlistment. In order to understand the way the residents of Woods lived their daily lives, it is necessary to understand the Jim Crow attitudes of Georgia and Florida at that time. Malinda Maynor, in her excellent work entitled "People and Place: Croatan Indians in Jim Crow Georgia, 1890-1920" published in the *American Indian Culture and Research Journal*, gives a detailed study of a settlement of Lumbee Indians who migrated to Bulloch County, Georgia to work the timber in 1890. The Lumbees remained there until about 1920 when the industry moved south to Florida. On July 27, 1899 the Bulloch herald reported on the interest of their timber companies in the possibility of making good money in northwest Florida;

> Manufacturers were elated by what they saw in the way of turpentine and timber prospects in Florida and reported that they may invest some money down that way.

Many Lumbee from Bulloch followed the timber down to Liberty in the late 1800's and the early part of the 1900's. Undoubtedly the same racial attitudes that these mixed-blood Indians faced in Georgia would also follow them down to Florida.

One example of the conditions faced by the inhabitants of Woods is demonstrated by a 1901 article which appeared in the May 24, 1901 Statesboro News. This article made mention of a young boy who had been murdered at a timber camp:

> The boy was about sixteen years old, and it is said was a part Indian. And like other good Indians, he is now dead.

Another family from Woods with strong ties to the home population of Cheraws in the Carolinas was the Oxendine family. Thanks to Mr. J. Oxendine, a friend from Robison County NC, for this biography concerning his relatives from the Cheraw Indians of North Florida Community at the Woods settlement.

> Elias Oxendine and Lawrence were both born in Robeson County, NC (Pembroke) in 1843 and 1872. Elias and his father James Jr. (first Indian County Commissioner) were probably among the most prominent families. There was a downturn in the economy in the early 1880's and some of the families left, including mine. Elias settled in Marianna in 1886. He brought 1,000 acres three miles west of Marianna (Aberdeen) and set up his sawmill and company store. He moved to Washington County, FL in 1900. He stayed in Marianna and raised a family of 11 children. My father and I were both born there. In 1943 my father moved to Tallahassee and stayed there until his death. -- I too was raised on the southside - Lake Bradford Road. He had 2 brothers Charles Jr. and Don (Courtland Duane).There were Oxendines (Elias' uncle's boys) that went to Liberty County, FL. Two brothers set up Oxendine Brothers Turpentine Company. In 1879, or so, Henry fell off his horse and died. His wife remarried. Henry's two boys stayed in Liberty County and are buried there.

More than likely all Oxendines are descended from one man born about 1694. He was listed as being a Mulatto. He was indentured for 30-years. By 1753 he was in

Robeson County, NC (was Bladen County back then). The authors have about 10,500 of his descendants (those that were born with the Oxendine name) listed. Hugh Everett Oxendine's father was Henry H. Oxendine. Henry fell off a horse in 1884 in Liberty County, Florida and was killed. Prior to his death Henry and his brother had opened up Oxendine Brothers Turpentine Company in Liberty County, Florida. After his father's death his mother Martha Ivey Goodman Oxendine married a man named Peacock. He, his brother Thomas and mother continued to live in Liberty County, FL.[1]

Henry Oxendine - White, Male. Henry died June 1884. He was 29 years old (born about 1855). He was married and was from North Carolina. His mother and father also were from North Carolina. His occupation was working in the turpentine industry. The cause of his death was "fall from horse." Attending physican was L.D. Carson.[2]

Vol 24, ED, 115, Sheet 5, Line 91, HH 142/145		
John Kever	37 (1883)	(Head, White, Wooding, can r/w)
Eddie Kever	24 (1896)	(Wife, White, Can r/w)
Iduma Kever	08 (1912)	(Dau, White)
Tharion Kever	06 (1914)	(Dau, White)
Eldle Mary Kever	04 (1916)	(Dau, White)
Harmon Kever	02 (1918)	(Son, White)
Hugh Oxendine	36 (1884) FL NC FL	(Roomer, White)
(Probably counted twice)[3]		

Hugh E. Oxendine 35 (1885) FL NC FL
(White)(Wooding on AN Railroad)
Source: Census Record: 1930 – Liberty County, Florida

---

[1] Census Mortality Schedule: 1885 – Liberty County, Florida

[2] Liberty County Mortality Schedule, 1885, Roll 7, Target 11, page 652.

[3] Census Record: 1920 - Liberty County, FL, Vol 24, ED 117, Sheet 2, Line 14, Vilas Pct 8

Vol 37, ED 39-2, Sheet 7B, Line 71, HH 138/138, Pct 2
Briston, 11 Apr, Owns house

Hugh Oxendine 47 (1883) FL NC FL (Head, White, Md
at 30, Can r/w, Farmer)
Martha L. Peacock 70 (1860) FL FL FL (Mother,
White, Widowed)
Source: Census Record: 1945 - Liberty County, Florida
Pct 2, Bristol, Inside city limits
Hugh Oxendine 63 (1882) FL (Head, White, Farmer)

Hugh Oxendine divorced Maggie (Oxendine) 1947,
Liberty County, Florida[4]

Hugh Everett Oxendine was born 15 Sep 1881, Liberty County, Florida. He died 25 Oct 1954, Chattahoochee, Gadsden, Florida. He left a will:

Last Will and Testament of Hugh Oxendine:

I, Hugh Oxendine, being of sound and deposing mind
and memory, but realizing the uncertainties of this life
do hereby make, declare and publish this to be my last
will and testament,

First: I will to my body a decent and honorable burial,
and hereby direct my administrator to pay the cost of
my last illiness and the cost of my burial from any
funds in my estate at the time of my death.

Second: To Hector O. Kever and Jane Kever, husband
and wife, I will and bequeath all the rest residue and
remainder of my estate, of every nature and kind,
whether real personal or otherwise, wherever situate,
share and share alike.

Third: I hereby designate and appoint Hestor O. Kever
and Jane Kever as administrators of this my last will
and testament, and direct that they serve without bond.

---

[4] Florida Divorce Index, 1927-2001, File number 20884

In witness whereof I have hereunto set my hand and seal at Bristol, Liberty County, Florida on this the 21st day of August 1954. //signed, Hugh Oxendine//

The above partly written and printed instrument was subcribed by the said Hugh Oxendine in our presence and acknowledged by him to each of us; and Hugh Oxendine at the same time declared the above instrument to be his last will and testament; and we at his request have signed our names as witness hereto in his presence and in the presence of each other and have written opposite our names our respective ... A.L. Suviens, residence Bristol Fla. witness. Alvin C. Weaver, residence Bristol, Fla. witness.

In: Court of County Judge, Liberty County, Florida. In probate, proof of will. Before me, the undersigned County Judge of said county. Cause A.L. Suveins and Alvin C. Weaver to me well known, who being duly sworn by me, depose and say that the Instrument exiibited to affiants as the last will and testament of Hugh Oxendine, deceased, is the same Instrument that afficants on the 21st day of August A.D. 1954. As attesting witnesses subscribed at the special instance and request of said testator, Hugh Oxendine, In said testators presence and in the presence of each other, then and there next after the said testator had signed his name thereto, and that the said testator then and there in the presence of said attesting witnesses freely and voluntarily signed and published the same as his last will and testament. Signed A.L. Suviens and Alvin C. Weaver. Sworn to and subscribed before me this 2nd day of November 1954, (Seal) R. Deason, County Judge, Liberty County, Florida.[5]

---

[5] Court Record: Liberty County, Florida, Will Book D, Page 34.

The following is an excerpt from the same book we looked at earlier in regards to the Porter family, *Sacred Grounds*, concerning the Oxendine family:

> OXENDINE The surname Oxendine is stereotypically Lumbee and readily identified in Bladen and Robeson records. It appears in Bladen tax lists of 1759, 1768, 1769, and the census of 1790, located west of Back Swamp, and east and northeast of Drounding Creek. John Oxendine lived on Pugh's bridge path in a grant to Thomas Fale 27 Aug. 1753. In 1753 and 1763 an Oxendine lived on a 100 acre tract north of Pugh's (Little Marsh) and moved southward to the east side of Drowning Creek next to land of Jacob Pittman and James Johnston Jr., before 14 July 1770 (Bladen County deeds, 1738-1779, 302-303) John was north of Little Marsh next to John Johnson Jr. 17 Aug. 1773. John, possibly John Jr., patented 100 acres east of Drounding Creek which included John Sr.'s improvements 5 March 1759. Cudworth Oxendine made improvements west of Back Swamp before 1778 on land later patented by John Bullard Jr. Charles Oxendine, listed as White in 1786, had 6 males, age 16-60, and 5 white females, living near Mark Broom. In the 1850 census of Robeson, family members reported having been born in Robeson as early as 1780, 1781, 1790, 1795, and numerous people of that name said they were born in Robeson in the early 1800's. Only one Oxendine reported being born elsewhere, Columbus County, in 1800. Tax collectors raised the ire of one Oxendine before 1790 in trying to list him as being "mixed blood." The 1801 tax list of Captain Watson's district shows Charles Oxendine, 100 acres and 1 free poll, and Jessey Oxendine with 135 acres and 1 free poll. Bryant Oxendine left a will dated 1831 (Will Book 1, 300). By 1830 there were eight Mulatoe families named Oxendine in the county and the name was self-identified as Indian on the 1900 census. Oxendine was listed as Indian on the 1930 census of Pembroke Town-

ship. Death records show the Indian name of Oxendine from 1916-1955 all over Robeson County but especially in Rowland Township.

They were found in Alfordsville, Burnt Swamp, Fairmont, Gatty, Pembroke, Raft Swamp, Red Springs, Rennert, and Smith's Townships. They are related to numerous other Lumbee families especially the Locklear family. The Lumbee name Oxendine was enrolled at Pembroke State University in 1924. Delton Oxendine served on the Lumbee Tribal Council in 2004. Hearl Oxendine ran for Tribal Council in 2004. Laure Oxendine was Miss Lumbee in 2004.

The Roots of the Hill Family in the Old Creek Nation

Though most of the families of what would become the Cheraw Indians of northern Florida were rooted in the eastern Siouan populations of the Carolinas, a few had other tribal roots as well, such as the Hill family. In March of 1829, three Creek Indian girls, all citizens of the Creek Nation, married three brothers from the Hill family of Union County South Carolina. Nancy, Sarah, and Amanda Doyle, all described as "Belles of the Creek Nation" by the South Carolina Marriage Index listings, married George, Alexander, and James Hill, three brothers stationed at Fort Mitchell, in the Creek Nation. The three young soldiers, George Robert Wesley, James Jr., and Alexander, joined the American Army in 1828. Nearby the Hill boys' duty station of Fort Mitchell, Creek Nation was a school for Indian Girls called the Asbury Missionary Institute, which the Hill family was already involved with. The Reverend Mister Hill, a relative of the boys, performed hundreds of marriages on this frontier during his time there. Eventually, George and Alexander left the area. They first moved to Decatur County, Georgia and then on to Jackson County

Florida, along with their Indian wives, Nancy and Sarah Doyle. Upon researching the oral histories passed through the various Hill family branches in Florida, as well as those in the Creek Nation in Oklahoma, we found indicators of where to search for the records. Amanda was the daughter of Nimrod Doyle, and Nancy and Sarah most likely his nieces, daughters of Edmond Doyle a Creek Nation trader with the Leslie, Panton, and Forbes Trading company.

During our research, we found a South Carolina Marriage Index Book at the Florida State Archives in the Capital Building Complex in Tallahassee Florida (the R. A. Gray Building), which listed an indexed reference to the marriages of these three couples. It seems from the documentary evidence that the Cherokee Phoenix, the national newspaper of the Cherokee Nation, as well as four other local Milledgeville, Georgia area newspapers, covered the weddings. It was said to be very extravagant for the times, according the article. Fort Mitchell was located on the frontier near where Creek Nation, Cherokee Nation, Georgia, and South Carolina met. Using the Index reference as a guide, we began to inquire about the possibility of one of the original newspapers that carried the article possibly being still in existence.

We were eventually able to secure a copy of it with the (much appreciated) assistance of the research staff at the Cherokee Nation of Oklahoma's Tribal Headquarters in Tahlequah, Oklahoma. Included in this chapter is the letter sent with the document. We also were able to gather several documents compiled by the Decatur County Georgia Historical Society that listed all the descendants of the George Hill- Nancy Doyle and Alexander Hill-Sarah Doyle marriages, which were many.

The following was recorded in Milledgeville, Georgia Newspaper Clippings (*Southern Recorder*), Volume II 1828-1832, by Tad Evans, found in the stacks of the Florida state Archives. Five other periodical sources in those stacks include an April 29 1829 edition (Volume 2 number 7) of the *Cherokee Phoenix*. The records show that on March 3 1829 the brothers Alexander, George, and James Hill, all from Darlington District in South Carolina and stationed at Fort Mitchell, Creek Nation, were married by the Reverend Mr. Hill, to Sarah, Nancy, and Amanda Doyle, Creek Indian girls attending the Asbury Missionary Institute. The details of this marriage were captured in the *Cherokee Phoenix* article from 1829:

> Married on the 3rd of March, at the Asbury Missionary Institute, near Fort Mitchell Creek Nation, by the reverend Mr. Hill, the Mr. James Hill of the US Army, to Miss Amanda Doyle, a Creek Pupil of the Institution. This establishment is under the charge of Mr. and Mrs. Hill, who were desirous of showing the natives how this ceremony is performed in a refined state of society, and the highest encomiums are due them for their entire success. Great exertion and ingenuity were necessary to accomplish it. The company consisted of about twenty white persons and one hundred and fifty natives. The bride and her two maids were dressed with great taste and propriety, according to the fashion of the age. The groom and his two associated were in full military costume; and those persons present accustomed to wedding scenes, pronounced this bridal party one of the handsomest they had ever witnessed.
>
> After the marriage ceremony, the happy pair were congratulated with all good wishes; cake and wine were passed around, and in due time a bountiful supper was partaken of by the whole company , and the evening passed on in the most agreeable manner possible. All parties seemed delighted with the occasion. A number of strangers present will never forget the kind and hos-

pitable reception given them by Mr. and Mrs. Hill.-Georgia Courier[6]

The indexed reference in the Milledgeville, Georgia Newspaper Clippings (*Southern Recorder*), Volume II 1828-1832 states:

> HILL, Mr. James of the US Army m. DOYLE, Miss Amanda, a Creek pupil of the Asbury Missionary Institution near Fort Mitchell Creek Nation, m. there 3-3-1829 by Rev. Mr. Hill. AC 3-18-1829; CP 4-29-1829; A th 4-7-1929; SP 3-21-1829; SR 4-21-1829. DG 4-19-1829 gives wedding date as 4-3-1829.

> HILL, Alexander of the US Army m. DOYLE, Miss Sarah, a belle of the Creek Nation, m. there 3-3-1829 State of Georgia CP 4-29-1829.

> HILL, George W. of the US Army m. DOYLE, Miss Nancy, a belle of the Creek Nation, m. there 3-3-1829 State of Georgia CP 4-29-1829.

This is a transcription of the "Alexander Hill" narrative, by Robert Earl Woodham, from *Decatur County, Ga. Past and Present 1823-1991*, a genealogy index compiled by the Decatur County Historical Society.

> The Hill Family has been in Seminole County since the 1830's. Several related Hill families moved to Spring Creek and nearby areas across the river in Jackson County (Florida). They came here from Darlington District, South Carolina.

> The first to settle here was Alexander hill Sr., who was born in 1812 and died in 1880. His wife's name is Unknown. She was the sister of the wife of his brother, George W Hill. Alexander had 7 children, all born at Spring Creek.

---

[6] *Cherokee Phoenix, 1929.*

Alex's son Ferdinand Hill was born in 1839 and died 6 May 1864 as a confederate soldier at the Battle of the Wilderness near Richmond VA.

Alex's daughters Lovie and Mahalia Caroline never married. Nothing is known of sons William and Richmond.

Alex's son Harmon Hill (1849) married Julia R. Minton 15 February 1877. Their children include Ella, Noah Lonzo, Emma, Luther D, Zenie, Jewel, and Meck (married to Cleveland Conyers)

Alexander Hill Jr. was born 1852 and died 1923. He and his wife Mary Ann (1852-1921) are both buried at Spring Creek. They had at least nine children: Marcus M. (1875-1904) married Mary Hall; Sophia Ann (1881), married Tully Murkison; Mathew D.; Rufus A. who married first Rhoda M.J. Thursby, and later to Annie Wilson; Mary; Preston Ulysses (1889-1964) who married first Corene Holt, then later Kate Shores; Alto E, who married James K Braswell; Alma S. (1893-1952) married to Joe Barber; and John C.

Alexander's brother, George Wesley Hill Sr. was born in 1804 in Darlington District South Carolina. His wife Nancy was the sister of Alexander's wife, making the two couples (descendents) double first cousins.

George moved from South Carolina to Spring Creek (Georgia) about 1856. He lived for several years at the intersection of Desser Road and Spring Creek Road. Nancy (born 1815) died about 1856 and is buried in a family plot at the intersection. They had at least 13 children.

George's son John A Hill was born in 1835; He married Mary Ann Dowell on 22 June 1852. He was a confederate soldier.

George's son Rueben Ezekiel Hill was born in 1836, he married Martha Frances Minton on 7 September 1865, and they had one daughter Rebecca.

George's son Thomas was born in 1838 and died on 12 November 1864 as a confederate soldier in a Yankee POW camp.

George's daughter Emma Elizabeth (1840) married Daniel Minton.

George's son Allen Hill (1842) married Amelia Conyers on 27 February 1868. They had one son, Asberry.

George's daughter Julia Hill (1844) married Waydon Hewitt.

A son, Dempsey Hill (1845) married Catherine McMillan on 18 August 1870. He lived in Jackson County (Florida)

A son, Johnathan H. Hill was born 2 February 1848 and died 18 October 1918. He married Nancy Melvina Summers; they had at least 14 children and lived at Grand Ridge (Jackson County, Florida)

William Cato (Cate) Hill (1853) married Caroline Bennett in 1872. Cate and Carrie had seven children and lived at Grand Ridge.

Susan Catherine Hill was born 24 December 1853 and died 29 August 1931. She was married to Moses F.J. Conyers.

George W Hill (1856) married first Caroline Conyers 2 February 1872. They had 2 children, James Wesley and Martha.

The generation's long saga of intermarriages among the above mentioned families and the other Indian families of the area of the Apalachicola River would be the nucleus of the Woods settlement. The Cheraw Indians of North Florida community of today is a complex one. We include copies of documents about the Hill family as an example of the multiple tribal origins of some of the Cheraw Indians of north Florida. Nevertheless, most of the families are of predominantly Catawba and Lumbee (Cheraw-Siouan) stock, with some, like the Hills from Creek ancestry. This small take on the Hill family is by no means nearly comprehensive or inclusive of the entirety of this branch of the Hill family, and their experience since leaving Creek Nation. As well there is a copy of the roll of Thlekatchka (Broken Arrow) Tribal Town of the Creek Nation that lists Nimrod, Jackson, and Muscogee Doyell as dwelling therein. These are the only persons on the 1832 Abbot-Parsons Roll (Creek Nation Removal Roll) with the surname Doyell and are the relatives of these three girls, Nancy, Sarah, and Amanda Doyle (Nimrods daughter), who were attending the missionary school at Fort Mitchell. A well-known historical figure in the decades after the war of 1812 who was heavily involved in the Creek and Seminole Nation intrigues of the times was Edmund Doyle, who is most likely the father of the "Creek Nation Belles" Nancy and Sarah, (albeit another possibility is Jackson Doyle).

Edmund established a trading outpost on the Apalachicola River and was part of the Leslie, Panton, and Forbes Company West Florida economic endeavors. He was licensed to trade with the Creek and Apalachicola Indians living in the area at the time. I have found numerous history book narratives about his involvement in the important events in west Florida and the control of the area struggles between the English, Spanish, and Americans as well as the Indian tribe's part in these dramatic events. He is listed in historical references as having an Indian wife and children and is probably the relative of the Doyell family at Thlekatchka (Broken Arrow).

He is known as well for having a price on his head by the Miccosukee chiefs, causing him and his family to have to retreat to a Lower Creek town for safety at one point, according to Seminole oral history. The trading post he founded became the famous Negro Fort, known to history as a stronghold, retreated to by hostile Blacks and Seminoles and destroyed along with three hundred partisans and their families who were inside. The massacre began with the first shot from Andrew Jackson's naval cannonade into the fort as his forces invaded Spanish Florida and engaged the poorly armed hostile Red Sticks. During the Civil War the Negro Fort was reconstituted as a confederate garrison and named Fort Gadsden, and fell soon thereafter to union forces. It has had many incarnations throughout the long history of Florida. It was bloodied ground on many occasions in the tumultuous journey of Florida to becoming American. Fort Gadsden is a state park today, and is near Apalachicola, Florida, a community located on the coast a few miles downriver from Blountstown. Research continues on the interconnections between the Doyle family and the Hill family. Nimrod Doyle, who would eventually be a Texas Ranger, along with his daughters Amanda and Muscogee moved to Texas after receiving land under the Treaty of Fort Jackson in Alabama. Amanda later wound up living in Eufaula Indian territory after years in Texas, where her family helped found the town of Sulphur Springs. Her nephew George Hill, son of Nancy Doyle Hill would move to Creek Nation as a young man taking an allotment. He would be appointed Chief in the 1920's, and have a large family.

Sources

- *Names in South Carolina* edited by Claude Henry Neuffer.Pg.XII:41

- *South Carolina Land Grants (1784-1830)* 160, vol. 32.R A Gray Library Private Collection, Florida State Archives, Tall. Fl

- *Early South Carolina Marriages* Vol.2 (1735-1885) implied in SC Law Reports, Union County

- *North and South Carolina Marriages 1800-1885* R A Gray Library Private Collection, Florida State Archives, Tall. Fl

- *Records of US Army enlistees (South Carolina) 1795-1850*

- *Federal Census of Georgia*: 1860 Decatur County, 1870 Decatur County

- *Federal Census of Florida*: 1860 Jackson County, 1870 Jackson County, 1885 Jackson County, 1870 Holmes Countym 1885 Holmes County

- *Decatur County Past and Present 1823-1991*, compiled by the Decatur County Historical Society and the Ellen Payne Odom Genealogical Library.

Milledgeville, Georgia, Newspaper Clippings
(Southern Recorder), Volume II 1828 - 1832

By

Tad Evans

These are scanned excerpts from the above-mentioned SC Marriage Index books from the Florida State Archives (stacks), in Tallahassee, Florida concerning the marriages of Nancy, Sarah, and Amanada Doyle to George, Alexander, and James Hill.

Elizabeth of Houston Co.
Esq. GJ 12-19-1826
HILL, Henry, murdered 11-1824 by Joseph S. Loring;
Loring escaped. Hill was a ferryman at Macon, Ga. GJM
12-1-1824 GSL
. HILL, Mr. James of the U.S. Army m. DOYLE, Miss
Amanda, a Creek pupil of Asbury Missonary Institution
near Ft. Mitchell, Creek Nation, m. there 3-3-1829 by Rev.
Mr. Hill. AC 3-18-1829; CP 4-29-1829; Ath 4-7-1829; SP
3-21-1829; SR 4-21-1829. DG 4-19-1829 gives wedding
date as 4-3-1829
HILL, Jeremiah m. SIKES, Mrs. Margaret in Tattnall Co. by

Lucy R., dau. of late Jeremiah Crocker of Hartford. Conn.
m. 8-3-1825 at Hartford by Rev. Mr. Cushman. GR
8-13-1825; DG 3-18-1825
HILL, Alexander of the U.S. Army m. DOYLE, Miss
Sarah a belle of the   Creek Nation. m. there 3-3-1829
State of Georgia. CP 4-29-1829
HILL, Frances Elizabeth Bailey, 6m 24d, only dau. of Eli S.
and C.M.S. Hill of Walton Co., d. 6-16-1827. SR 6-25-1827
d. 6-16-1827. SR 6-25-1827.
HILL, George W. of the U.S. Army m. DOYLE, Miss
Nancy a belle of the   Creek Nation, m. there 3-3-1829
CP 4-29-1829.
HILL, Rev. George, d. 8-22-1829 in Milledgeville,
"Stationed Preacher of the Methodist Church." He entered

lung on that station; ...en obliged to hang ...attempting to take brig. The Officer it they had informa- r piratical vessels cruizing off Cape ed Capt. P. to give birth. The Capt. of not inquire how ma- taken, but supposed been at least from he crew of the brig nen, and carries 18 had given the above lavit. rn by a gentleman, Jen. Gadesden, that il at Havana had in- ...ican Commercial ...mation had been ana, that the French of Bordeaux, Capt. vessel sailed from ch, for Havana, was f the American ship n, within 5 miles of totally abandoned. ks of Merchandize ...ere scattered about ...h were also stained gave every reason to ...v had been murder- The L'Amedee was attied into New Or- jamin Morgas. ...also states that an ...made by a Spanish ...was fortunately frus- ...rate the intendant of ...the above, we learn

Married on the 3d of March, at the Asbury Missionary Institution, near Fort Mitchell, Creek Nation, by the Rev. Mr. Hill, Mr. James Hill of the U. S. Army, to Miss Amanda Doyle, a Creek pupil of the Institution.— This establishment is under the charge of Mr. and Mrs. Hill, who were de- sirous of showing the natives how this ceremony is performed in a refined state of society, and the highest enco- uniums are due them for their entire success. Great exertion and ingeni- ty were necessary to accomplish it.— The company consisted of about twen- ty white persons and one hundred and fifty natives. The bride and her two maids were dressed with great taste and propriety, according to the fash- ion of the age. The groom and his two associates were in full military costume; and those persons present, accustomed to wedding scenes, pro- nounced this bridal party one of the handsomest they had ever witnessed. After the marriage ceremony, the hap- py pair were congratulated with all good wishes; cake and wine were pass- ed round, and in due time a bountiful supper was partaken of by the whole company, and the evening passed off in the most agreeable manner possi- ble. All parties seemed delighted with the occasion. A number of stran- gers present, will never forget the kind and hospitable reception given them by Mr. and Mrs. Hill.—Geor- gia Courier.

...school is advertised in Charles Wickliffe, ... of a Kentucky paper, ... manslaughter. There evidence to warrant th a higher crime.

Gold.—The Fayette er, of the 13th inst. say in this state is enlarged almost every day. W cious article has lately ral places near Cartha about 40 miles from thi

It seems that the gan Mr. Stephenson in Sa glad to escape from Ne skins, instead of the re this country and 1000l. er it was their design to

The Bennington, Vt third wife who has been treatment of her husba died last week. It is int perance was the moving

Cherokee Phoenix 8

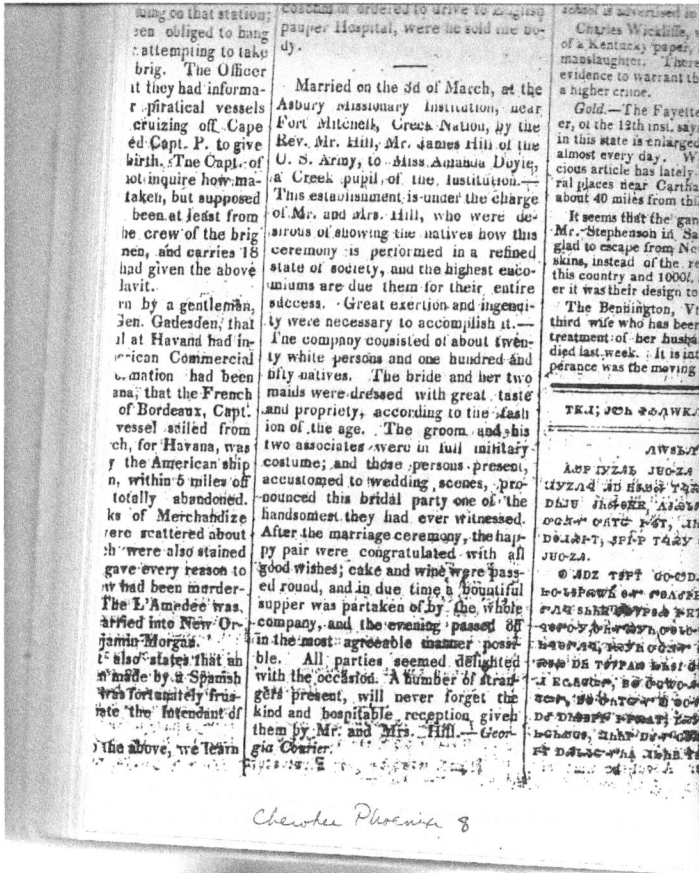

Article from the 1829 Cherokee Phoenix that documents Doyle to Hill family marriages.

American Native Press Archives

September 22, 1999

Mr. Chris Sewell
11625 E. 83rd St. N.
No. BB
Owasso, OK 74055

Dear Mr. Sewell:

Enclosed is a printout from the Cherokee Phoenix. I found it on my
desk under a pile of papers. Did I send a copy of it to you? If
not I apologize for not getting it out, for I copied it shortly after
we spoke by telephone.

This is the only reference that I found in our index to the Cherokee
Phoenix. However, there are about two years still to go on the
indexing, and something may turn up yet. News of Asbury Mission shows up
now and then, so I will look at those items carefully. If anything
new shows up, I will copy it and send along.

Good searching!

Sincerely,

Daniel F. Littlefield, Jr.
Archives Director

University of Arkansas at Little Rock • 502 Stabler Hall • 2801 S. University • Little Rock, AR 72204-1099 • (501) 569-3160/FAX-569-8373

Chief Buck Bryant, grandson of Noah Hill
Blountstown Fl.

Tony Davis, Florida Cheraw

The Family of Daniel Minton Jr. and Hattie Tipton,
Seated at right is Martha Emma Hill, the granddaughter
George W. Hill and Nancy Doyle, a citizen of the Creek
Nation. They are pictured in Woods, Florida circa 1920.

Even at its height, Woods was not quite large enough
to be called a town. At its prime it consisted of about 14
homes, a one-room school, and a small merchandise store,
which was operated by the Hill family. According to the
residency claims of individual birth and marriage records,
the community became physically known as Woods some-
time around 1915. By the beginning of World War Two, the
physical landmark buildings had fallen out of use, and today have mostly fallen away and are surrounded by dense
growth.

The Liberty County Courthouse was the victim of
repeated fires both before and after 1940, and the County
was unable to maintain any historic records prior to the
Second World War, which makes it hard to find documentary evidence of the daily relations of the Woods community with their surrounding White and Black neighbors.
Mary Brown Kever, the wife of Frank Kever originally

from France, was a woman of Catawba descent, who lived in the Woods settlement. Concerning Mary Brown and her origins, my grandfather Ray Kever, her grandson, was a man who was very full-blood Indian in his physical appearance. Several times through the years he would say to me:

> My grandmother Mary Brown was an Indian from South Carolina and moved here with her French-speaking husband, a Whiteman. She was buried outside the White part of the Bristol Cemetery (in Liberty County, Florida) because they wouldn't let her be buried in the White part of the cemetery.

The following is an excerpt concerning the migration of his family from South Carolina to Florida sent to us by Professor Bloom, and is excerpted from the "Family Sketches" section of the book *Catawba Indian Genealogy* by Ian Watson, printed in 1995 as a part of the *Papers in Anthropology*, from the State University of New York. (ISBN 0-9617915-3-5):

> Jamey Brown was living as early as 30 Nov. 1810 when he signed a petition (g1810), and was listed in the Plat Book under dates from 11 May 1813 to July 1819 (PB, 115). He was dead by September 1820 when his widow Sally took his rents (PB, 111). Sally, sometimes called Sarah, was living as late as 1824 (PB 107). She was assigned rents with Billie Ayers once (PB 106), which suggests she may be the same person as Suzy Ayres who I list above among early, unconnected Browns. Jamey himself took rents for Prissy Bullen in 1816 (PB 175) Sally received rents for Jamey Browns children in Dec 1822 (PB 111,114), but their names are not known. Several lucky chances allow us to learn the identity of Sally Brown. A strange note in the plat Book (p.114) reads: "Quincy West Florida Apalachicola District Jamey Brown Catawba Indian intermarried with a Pamunkey Pocahontas." We can interpret "Pocahontas" as

a derogatory term for a Pamunkey woman, and not indicative of her actual name. So, checking the Murshes—The Pamunkey family who joined the Catawbas in the early 1800's—We find that Sarah Mursh, the daughter of Robert and Elizabeth Mursh, was born 29 March 1790, was 28 and called Sally in 1820, and, as Sarah Brown, testified to her mother's claim for a pension on 16 January 184{last number unreadable} (M01).

Another resident in Woods settlement with strong ties to both Scott Town and Scott's Ferry families was Mary Samantha Blanchard Dasher (the daughter of John Blanchard and Ellen Scott of Scott's Ferry), the wife of Emmitt Dasher. The Hill family also had many students enrolled at the Marysville School at Scott's Ferry (see appendix). Oral history from Sallie Kever, who was very active as an Indian leader in Liberty County in the latter half of her life and was the daughter of Nellie Hill Whittaker, said that there were several ties between these same to communities that were generally unknown due to illegitimacy issues.

Mary Porter attended the Cherokee Indian Normal School, Robeson County, NC

Ray and Sallie Kever, both born in Woods, Florida

With the exhaustion of the hardwoods along the Apalachicola in the 1940's, the majority of the Woods Communities inhabitants spread out to individual homesteads in western Liberty and other surrounding counties. This also occurred in the larger related settlements of Scott Town and Scott's Ferry. The dispersion of population from the clustered settlements would only accelerate in the decades to come with desegregation. In the documentary record, several Cheraw men, including Noah Hill from the Woods Community, are recorded on their WW I Civil Enlistment cards under the race block as Caucasian and Indian, with the checkmark being in the *citizen* rather than *the non-citizen* box under the Indian "racial" category. In his recent book *Those Who Remain; A Photographers Memoir of South Carolina Indians*, Gene J. Crediford stated:

> On June 2, 1924, Congress passed the Citizenship Act of 1924, which states that "all non-citizen Indians born within the territorial limits of the United States be, and they are hereby, declared to be citizens of the United States: provided that the granting of such citizenship shall not in any manner impair or otherwise affect the

right of any Indian to tribal or other property" (U.S. Code, Title 8, sec. 1401 [a][2]). In this context a non-citizen Indian means, as I understand it, a person who is a member of a federally recognized tribe; in other words, citizen Indians were at the mercy of state laws in that era.

As we have seen from the many court cases and social incidents regarding the school and military enlistment situations in the first half of the twentieth century we have reviewed earlier, north Florida's Cheraw people were definitely at the mercy of state laws of the time.

Noah Hill, of the Woods Community

Essie Hill Bryant with her daughter Louise Bryant and
son Billie (Buck) Bryant
Essie was the daughter of Noah Hill

Annie Bass Love and Louise Bryant Tipton. Woods, Florida circa 1970.

Lloyd Hill with wife and children, to his right is his father-in-law

Inez Scott and family | Jim and Wesley Scott

George Scotts WWI 1918 Civil Enlistments, Caucasian-Indian listed as "race"

9. "Claim to be part Spanish and Indian" Other Florida Groups of Cheraw Ancestry

The Carolina Cheraw Origins of the Dominickers

Hall, Thomas, Bland, Forehand, Simmons, Mainer, Chavis, Mayo, Stephens

Dominicker was a pejorative term applied to several (interrelated) populations of mixed bloods across the panhandle, most often used in Walton and Holmes Counties. We are currently working on an exhaustive research project, showing the differing lines of descent for the Mt. Zion community population as well as the historic Sam Story Euchee mixed blood families group (Potters, Harris, Fennell, and others). Both groups lived in the same area and held third-race statuses under segregation. They are often thought of as a single population, but were not intermarried groups to any appreciable degree during the segregation era. For now, I have gathered up some records and family sources about the so-called Dominicker people.

Currently several families who are or descend from the historic populations, including the Simmons, Hall, and Thomas families of Mt Zion School and community area are active in local Indian activities in somewhat of a political nature. Most of the descendants of the historic Dominicker community in Walton County, and to some degree Holmes County, are averse to admitting their ancestry, though a few are active in local and pan-Indian activities. Some are part of a local group known as the Echota Cherokee tribe. One person who descends from the historic community and is involved in the modern Indian community is Rodney Ryals. He is a descendent of the Simmons and other families, and active in the Ponce De Leon/ Defuniak Springs, Florida area with the Creeks (Muscogee Nation of Florida), formerly called Florida Tribe of Eastern Creek Indians. The former Chairman of this organization was John Thomas. His niece Ann Denson Tucker is chairwoman now. Below are some historical documents about the origins of these families.

1840 taxation census of Walton County, West Florida (later split to form Holmes)

Page 2:
Betsy Allen, 2 male FPOC, 4 female FPOC

Page 7:
Henry Stephens, 1 white female, 16 male FPOC
Alfred Mayo, 8 male FPOC, 4 female FPOC

1847 Walton County tax list:

William Chavers (sic Chavis),.$3.00, free man of color
Wiley Hall, $6.00, free man of color

Note: Wiley Hall would have been taxed double only if his wife was also a FPOC

1850 census Walton County:

Household #109: Hall, Wiley, age 45, farmer, born NC
Catherine, age 40, born NC
Wesley, 8, GA
Mary, 6, FL
James, 4, FL
Margaret, 2, FL

1855 Walton tax list:

Daniel Gunn....$3.30.............free man of color
Jonathan Manor (sic Mainer)...free man of color
Benj. Thomas...$3.30..........free man of color

These mixed-blood families with surnames of Allen, Mayo, Chavers, Hall, Mainer, and Thomas can be found in the 1810-1820 census of Northampton, NC, on the site of the Meherrin reservation. The specific names of Hall and Thomas are on documents relating to lease/sale of Meherrin reservation property.

The following paragraph is an origin legend as recounted in the Florida volume of the *Federal Writers Project* in the late 1930's. In the second paragraph below, the present authors respond in bold italics to the legend. Our response is based on the documentary record:

[Writers Project original] The beginning of the Dominicker Settlement was before the Civil War in 1855 by a black man named Joe Thomas. A slave raised a family of four children one boy and three girls, by a white woman named Polly Thomas. She owned the black man and after her husband was killed she took her slave for a husband and raised the four children. Their son Berrian Thomas married a white woman named Rally Hall. Their daughter named Martha Thomas married a white man named Bill Bland. The other girls raised a family of children without being married for different colored men.

[As corrected from the documented record] The beginning of the Dominicker Settlement was before the Civil War in 1855 [*In fact, Benjamin Thomas' family was on the 1850 census, so had to have arrived prior to 1855.*] by a black man named Joe Thomas [*In fact, the progenitor of the Thomasses was named Benjamin.*]. A slave [*In fact, Benjamin Thomas was taxed as a free man of Color, so obviously was not a slave.*] raised a family of four children one boy and three girls, by a white woman named Polly Thomas [*In fact, Benjamin's wife was named Jane.*]. She owned the black man [*Once again, Benjamin was never a slave.*] and after her husband was killed she took her slave for a husband (*In fact, this would have been illegal under Florida law. She, the slave, and the minister would have been whipped and the marriage annulled.*] and raised the four children. Their son Berrian Thomas married a white woman named Rally Hall [*Berrian Thomas married Mary Hall*]. Their daughter named Martha Thomas married a white man named Bill Bland. The other girls raised a family of children without being married for different colored men.

The 1850 Census of Homes Co.:

Household:
#109: George W. Mayo (son of Alfred Mayo), wife and 2 kids
#110: Jane Thomas (wife of Benjamin Thomas), 5 children
#111: Micajah Stephens (son of Henry Stephens), wife and 3 children
#112: Alfred Mayo, wife and 5 children
Note: Alfred Mayo would lead a mixed-blood wagon train to Louisiana and settle among other mixed-bloods there to form what would later be called the *Red Bones*.

The 1870 Census of Holmes county:

Household #320: Thomas, Berrian, 45, Male, "M", GA

Mary K, 34,"W", ALA
Christian A., 5 (female) "W", FL
Hall, James M., 13, "M", FL
Benjamin F., 10, "M", FL
Ruth J., 8,"M", FL

Household #321: Hall, Ann C, 62, "W", GA
Elizabeth M., 20, "W", ALA
Amelia A., 18, "W", ALA
Willis F., 16, "W", ALA

Household #322: Thomas, Mary, 38, "W", GA
Mary J., 8, "W", FL
Sarah F., 6, "W", FL
Franklin, 1, "W", FL

Household #323: Bland, William, 32, "W", FL
Martha, 33, "M", FL
Clara J., 13, "M", FL
June E., 4,"M", FL
William B., 2,"M", FL

1880 Holmes county census:

Household #142: Hall, Jeff, INDIAN, 34, FL
Catherine, "B", 30, FL

Note: census taker instructions for 1880 stated that only people of "predominantly Indian blood residing on known Indian reservations, or persons of unmixed Indian blood should be recorded as Indian."

Household #208: Hall, James, "W", 23, FL
Alice, "W", 23, FL
Mary, "W", 1, FL

Household #209: Thomas, Berry, "Mu", 57, GA
Mary, "W", 43, ALA
Christian,"Mu", 16 (grand-daug), FL
Hall, Benjamin, "W", 21 (step-son), FL

Household #210: Forehand, Sarah (Thomas), "Mu", 52, GA

John, "Mu", 19, FL
Horace, "Mu", 15, FL

Household #211: Bland, William,"W", 34, FL
Martha,"Mu", 44, GA
Clara,"Mu", 21, FL
Ginnie, "Mu", 15, FL
William, "Mu", 13, FL
Viola,"Mu", 9, FL
John,"Mu", 4, FL
Sarah, "Mu", 1, FL
Hall, Sarah (Niece), "Mu", 15, FL
Franklin (Nephew), "Mu", 13, FL

1885 Holmes County census:

Dwelling: 531, Hall, James M., "W", 25
Alice M, "W", 26
Mary J.,"W", 6
Coburn, "W", 4
Margaret, "W", 2
Arquilla, "W", 45, Aunt

532, Thomas, Benjamin,"Mu", 60
Christian A.,"Mu", 19, daughter

533, Bland, Martha,"Mu", 44
Clara J.,"Mu", 28
Jennie, "Mu", 18
William, "Mu", 16
Viola, "Mu", 14
John, "Mu", 9
Ailsy Ann, "Mu", 4
Forehand, Sarah,"Mu", 55, sister
Harris, "Mu", 19
Thomas, Sarah,"Mu", 18, niece

534, Forehand, John, "Mu", 23
Pallis, "W", 30
Mary, "Mu", 9
Lettice, "Mu", 5

Harris, Jr., "Mu", 11/12

535, Mayo, William,"Mu", 35
Margaret, "W", 30
Melvin, Catherine,"W", 4, niece

The primary families in the Dominicker community were Hall, Thomas, Bland (White man married a Thomas), Forehand (White man married a Thomas), and Simmons, as the documentation present shows. The family name of Simmons did not marry in until quite late (after 1880). Specifically after the Simmons man (censused as a "Mu" farm laborer in Dale Co, AL, then as Indian in Washington Co, FL) came in. This individual's Simmons family connects back to the Simmons' of Sampson Co, NC.

The following are transcripts of two unpublished, anonymous articles written for the Florida volume of the *Federal Writers Project*. The original typescripts are in the library of the University of Florida at Gainesville, from which these transcriptions were taken. The two narratives below are articles published in 1939 in the Florida volume of the *Federal Writer's Project State Guide Series*.

1939 Writers Project Narratives

PONCE DE LEON, 45.2m (64 alt, 382 pop), is the site of Ponce De Leon Springs, one of the many fountains of youth named for the Spanish explorer. In adjacent back country live "Dominickers," part Negro and part white, whose history goes back to the early 1860s. [Origin story #1A—Thomas family] Just before the War Between the States, Thomas, a white, lived on a plantation here, with his wife, two children, and several Negro slaves. After his death his wife married one of the slaves, by whom she had five children. As slaves often took the name of their masters, her Negro husband was also known as Thomas. Of the five children, three married whites, two married Negroes. Today their numerous descendants live in the backwoods, for the most part in poverty. The men are of good physique, but the women are often thin and worn in early life. All have large families, and the fairest daughter may have a brother distinctly Negroid in appearance. The name originated, it is said, when a white in suing for a divorce described his wife as "black and white, like an old Dominicker chicken." Dominicker children are not permitted to attend white schools, nor do they associate with Negroes. About 20 children attend a one-room school. As no rural bus is provided, he pupils often walk several miles to attend classes. An old cemetery, containing a large number of Dominicker graves, adjoins the school. Numerous curves and steep hills make driving west of Ponce de Leon somewhat dangerous; care and caution are advised.

Excerpted from the Federal Writers' Project (Fla.). *Florida: A Guide to the Southernmost State.* Sponsored by the State of Florida, Department of Public Instruction. New York: Oxford University Press, 1939.

The Dominicker Settlement

The Dominecker [sic] Settlement is located in Holmes County, about half way between Westville and Ponce de Leon, Florida. Westville prides itself on being the one that made bootleg liquor famous, and the Domineckers owned and operated the stills. Ponce de Leon is a small village -a trading post for farmers. During the time that lumber and turpentine were leading industries, the town thrived. Now, a small sawmill employs a few people and cull lumber is shipped to the paper mill at Panama City. People trade one product for another and there is very little money spent. The town derives its name from a small spring on the Pea River, called Ponce de Leon Springs. The spring claims to be the original Fountain of Youth discovered by Ponce de Leon. The Domineckers live in their little settlement and have few outside interests. The children are not allowed to attend the white schools. For a child from the settlement to attend school was unheard of until 10 years ago. Their efforts to enter their children in school caused such an upheaval [that] the school board finally compromised by establishing a grammar school for them. A few exceptions have been made in Westville for high school students, but they are never allowed to actually graduate. Two families have moved to Shamrock, Florida to send the children to a white school.

The Domineckers attend the Mt. Zion Baptist Church. It is supposed to be a white church, they are allowed to go to any church to preaching but cannot take a part in church affairs. They seldom attend any services but their own -unless it is a holiness revival. These people are sensitive, treacherous, and vindictive. They never start a disturbance but if any one bothers them – the whole family will do childish things to get revenge, to steal a hog or mutilate a crop is as good as a want. They are pathetically ignorant and an entire family will work hard for little compensation. The Domineckers come to town once a week for supplies. Their dilapidated wagons are drawn by anemic looking oxen. Each wagon is literally spilling over with children. Thay attend their business quickly and quietly and leave as unceremoniously as they came. They are treated with the same courtesy that a Negro receives—never served at a public fountain nor introduced to a white person. It would be ridiculous to prefix "Mr." or "Mrs." to their names. The Domineckers differ in size but they are practically the same type. Their skin is dark, swarthy and thick looking; some have medium skin with big brown freckles, their eyes are brown and sharp, usually deep-set.

They have beautiful white teeth and bright pink gums. Most of them have black straight hair, none of them have real kinky hair and one family has three children that are decided blonds—their skin looks sun-burned. They are a type of people that age quickly, probably

from lack of care. The men are big and burly looking,
noted for their strength and famous for halter-breaking
calves and horses.

The women are low in stature, fat and shapeless, they
wear loose-fitting clothes and no shoes. One woman 74
years of age has never owned a pair of shoes. When a
person is the smaller type his is almost dwarf-like in
size. There seems to be no in-between size. The people
move from one hut to another, often living alone for
awhile and then moving back into the family group.
Men, women and children work in the fields. Some
houses are scrupulously clean while others are filthy.
They just live from day to day -certainly not an ambi-
tious group. Each generation marries into the lower
class of white people; their original group will soon be
extinct. Common law marriage is practiced, as a matter
of fact -most of them take-up with each other. Local
people claim that the Domineckers are 95% Negro.
This statement is absurd. They are about three fourths
white and one eighth Negro and one eighth Indian.

The following unpublished article, from the informa-
tive archive on the rich past of the Florida panhandle including the Dominicker Community is from Mr. Hood. A
rich collection of information is maintained by Mr. Hood,
and is reproduced here by kind permission of Mr. Beale,
formerly employed by the U. S. Public Health Service and
the U. S. Census Bureau. The report was written as part of
his field notes during a research visit to Florida.

Beale's Report from 1956: A Visit to the Dominicker Mixed-Racial Group in Holms County, Florida

November 28, 1956

By Calvin Beale

I first went to Bonifay, the county seat, and visited the
county health nurses, Mrs. Lee and Mrs. Sims. They
immediately mentioned the letter of inquiry from Dr.

Witkop of Public Health Service and asked if I had any connection with it. I allowed as how I did. Both were glad to talk about the Dominicker group. Only one family is among their current patients. The patient is an elderly man, Jim Simmons, who has diabetes. The nurses, especially Mrs. Sims, a native of the county, knew other Dominickers. The term Dominicker is not acceptable to the group and is not used in their presence. They do not wish to be considered colored. One became very angry with Mrs. Lee when she, not knowing the family, listed a new-born child as Negro because of the somewhat Negroid appearance of the family. I believe she changed the record after the protest. The appearance of the group was said to be variable. Jim Simmons claims to be part Spanish and Indian. The nurses knew of the Forehand, Goddin (the present spelling), and Thomas families but had not been sure of the connection until I confirmed it. They also mentioned a Curry family. The names were all said to be held by white people too. The teeth of the Dominicker children were said to be better than the average for white children. There is no dentist in the county.

Some in the group suffer from TB. The group extends over into Walton County, where a couple of children in one family have a congenital malformation. (There is a Negro family in Holmes family [sic] with three albino children. I did not get the spelling of the name, which sounded like Hodah or Hoodah.) The nurses knew nothing of the origin of the Dominickers. They said Jim Simmons was approachable and probably would be glad to talk. All in the group were said to be poor. A separate elementary school is still maintained for the group, called the Mt. Zion School. Current enrollment is 12, said once to have been about 25. The nurses estimated the population of the group at 40. I next visited the Soil Conservationist, who knew of the group, but, not being a county native, took me to the man in charge of the Selective Service office. The S.S. man went over some of the same ground covered by the nurses. He said the Dominickers were sensitive on the race question and might not get information unless the questioner were referred in by someone accepted by the group.

It was his opinion that the children attending Mt. Zion school were essentially the darker ones and that some of those who looked white were in surrounding white schools. The teacher of the separate school is a white woman, Miss (?) Dupree, who lives in Westville. The present building was erected after World War II at a cost of $8,000. The S.S. man did not know how the Dominickers were drafted racially during World War II. Some farm, others work in forest industries. He said they were low in culture

The Mount Zion Community School, known locally as The Dominicker School (photo courtesy of Mr. Hood, a scholar and archivist of northern Florida's history)

Euchee Chief Sam Story and his Descendants in Walton County Florida

Potter, Fennel, Harris, Rowe

Euchee Chief Sam Story is a local legend with the rural families in the Walton and Holmes County area and has hundreds of descendants there, most of whom are assimilated into the local White and black population. In the Euchee Valley area most children grow up with tales of Chief Sam Story. He was Chief of a band of Euchee Indians in the early 1800s, a group who occupied the lands on and to the west of the Choctawhatchee River and the surrounding area The Euchee were originally in the Savannah area of Georgia but some had migrated to Florida and established several towns there, separate from the main body of Euchee who were settled in Creek Nation. This area of Florida, which would one day be Walton County, was sparsely populated and isolated much longer than other parts of the panhandle. When the first White settlers came into the area, the Euchee were doing well running cattle to Pensacola and trading with passing ships. Chief Story was friendly to the incoming American settlers and had good relations with them all his life. Some believe that his parents were Timothy Kinnard, a White man of Scottish descent, and an unknown Euchee woman, but this is in need of more scholarly research and has not been established documentarily. The chief was a well-known figure in the drama of the settlement of the Florida Panhandle and was respected by White settlers as forthright and fair dealing. In his elderly years more settlers had migrated to the area in ever-increasing numbers, this following the acquisition of the Florida territory by the United States through treaty from Spain in 1821, and a steady growing pressure was exerted on the resources of the Florida Euchee.

Around 1820, Neill McLennan and his brother-in-law, Daniel Campbell moved from the area near Richmond County in North Carolina. They came to the area that would become Walton County, Florida seeking a better life as many settlers after them would. These newcomers were invited by Chief Sam Story to settle on lands adjoining his village located on Bruce Creek in the Euchee Valley, near

the modern rural hamlets of red bay and Bruce. These settlers met the Chief in Pensacola when he was there engaged in trading and selling his cattle to the ships supply
traders in business there. After becoming friends, the men
and Chief Story were known to visit and assist each other,
and the men were joined by their families, other relatives
and friends. By the early 1830's many White people had
moved into the Euchee tribal area and were destroying for-
est resources depended on by the Indians, and were scaring
off the deer and other wildlife depended on by the Euchee
hunters. Tensions were growing across the frontier, often
disrupting the age old trade agreements and alliances
among the Indian communities. Both the McLennan family
as well as the old Chief decided to leave the area due to
these unwanted conditions.

The Euchee Chief sent a party to scout for lands to
the southeast, following news of relatives who were among
the Seminole in the south Florida wilderness. So while
many of the McLennan and their relatives decided to head
west by boat, and would later become prominent early settlers of what would become McLennan County, Texas, the
Euchee agreed that it was time to leave the increasingly
hostile social situation of the panhandle. Incursions by hostile Red-Stick Creek were making the area dangerous for
all Indians. Unfortunately, Chief Sam Story died just before
his tribe moved, and is buried south of the fork of Bruce
Creek and the Choctawhatchee River. After the traditional
time of mourning, several hundred Euchee went southward
to the coast of the Gulf of Mexico, traveling from Story's
Landing, located near the burial site of the chief, southeast
of Red Bay in Walton County. The main portion of the tribe
then traveled southeastward, traveling both by land and by
water to their new home among their Seminole kinsmen.
Nothing more was heard of them, but some descendants' of
the family speak of visitation among the Florida Euchee

descendants in the panhandle with relatives from south Florida, as well as with Oklahoma kin through the years. Most of the descendants of the Chief eventually settled with the Seminole Tribe in South Florida. It is well known from archival records and interviews with Oklahoma Euchee friends from Duck Creek Ceremonial Grounds and the Yuchi Tribal Organization (and the E.U.C.H.E.E. organization in Sapulpa, Oklahoma) that the United States Army forced some of the Walton County Euchee people and several other small West Florida bands to relocate west of the Mississippi River, in the Indian Territory.

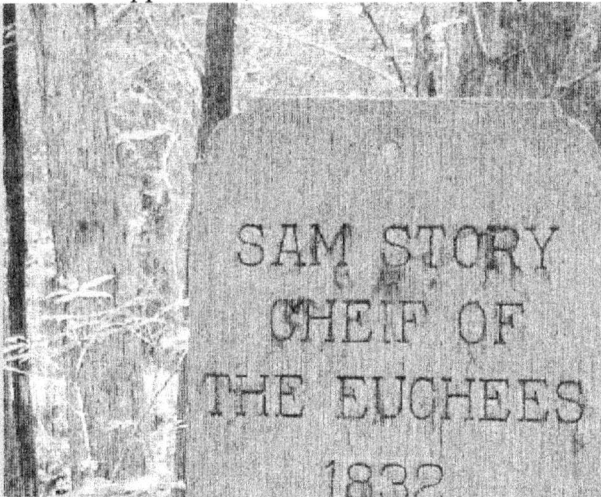

SAM STORY
CHEIF OF
THE EUCHEES
1832

CUDOS to Wanda Hewett Jewell, Hampton R. Campbell and Diane Merkel of the "Walton County History Detectives" for sharing this photo. Visit them at WaltonCountyHeritage@cox.net -- there's a lot of great history there!

This photo is of the monument at the burial place of Chief Story and is courtesy of the above individuals at WaltonCountyHeritage@cox.net

According to local traditional oral histories, Chief Sam Story had three sons, Jim Crow, Swift Hunter and Sleeping Fire, and three daughters, Leaping Water, Quiet Water and Round Water. Jim Crow, and many other members of the tribe, left numerous descendants, some of them have been confused with the Dominickers, a neighboring mixed-race group, by the surrounding White population of the times in Walton, Holmes, and Washington counties. Today the descendants are members of various local Indian groups in the panhandle, with the majority absorbed by the local White and black population. There were Euchee people in movement all over the southeast in the colonial era, and after the movement of the majority of the Walton County Euchee to the southern part of the Florida peninsula, they became a large band under Sam Story's grandson called Euchee Billy, and lived at a place called Spring Garden in Volusia County. Today many of the Florida Seminole are unaware of their connections to the Euchee people of Walton County, according to Mary Frances Johns, a Miccosukee elder. As representatives of the Florida Indian community, the authors often visit with Euchee people at Duck Creek Euchee Ceremonial Grounds in Oklahoma and the Euchee Tribe of Indians headquartered in Sapulpa, Oklahoma. We have shared our records and oral history with them in their recent effort to gain federal recognition as a separate Nation from the Creek Nation by the US government. Despite many descendants of Chief Sam Story's Band of Euchee today being assimilated into the general population of Walton County, or part of the local Creek and Cheraw tribal groups, his legend remains strong in his homeland among Indians and others alike.

Sources

John Love McKinnon, *History of Walton County.* Atlanta: Byrd Printing, 1911. Electronic version created 2002 by the State University System of Florida, pp. 62-66, 94-97. [1]

E. W. Carswell, *Holmesteading: The History of Holmes County, Florida*, published by the author at Chipley, Florida, 1986 (available in print only)

Clayton Gillis Metcalf, *Scots and Their Kin*, Volume I: Gilli(e)s, Padgett, Arrant, McQuagge, McLennan, published at Enterprise, Alabama, 1984 (available in print only)

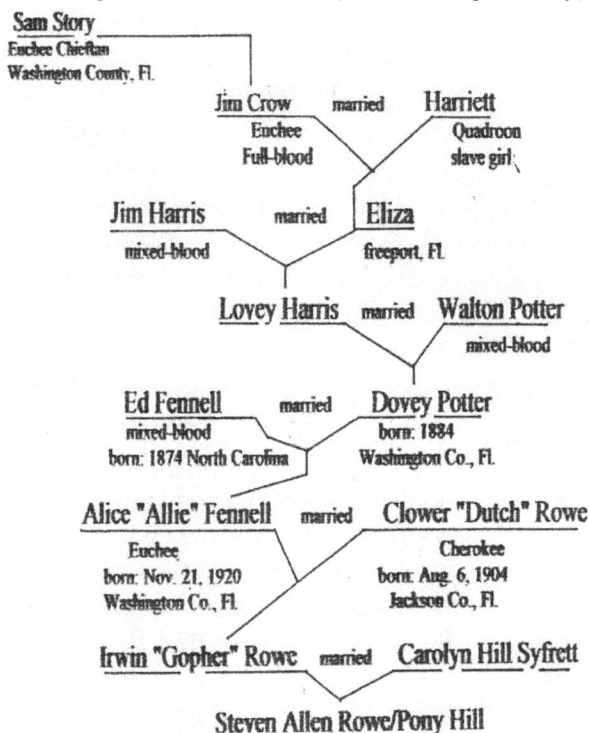

Sam Story
Euchee Chieftan
Washington County, Fl.

Jim Crow   married   **Harriett**
Euchee   Quadroon
Full-blood   slave girl

Jim Harris   married   **Eliza**
mixed-blood   freeport, Fl.

Lovey Harris   married   **Walton Potter**
                               mixed-blood

Ed Fennell   married   **Dovey Potter**
mixed-blood   born: 1884
born: 1874 North Carolina   Washington Co., Fl.

Alice "Allie" Fennell   married   **Clower "Dutch" Rowe**
Euchee   Cherokee
born: Nov. 21, 1920   born: Aug. 6, 1904
Washington Co., Fl.   Jackson Co., Fl.

Irwin "Gopher" Rowe   married   **Carolyn Hill Syfrett**

Steven Allen Rowe/Pony Hill

Pony Hill, Blountstown Cheraw leader, is a direct descendent of Sam Story on his father's side, whose genealogy is shown above

Steven Pony Hill (with cap) along with Harjo and Chris
Sewell at the Poarch Creek Indian reservation in 1996.
Pony is from Blountstown Florida. His father Irwin Rowe
is from Walton County, and is a descendent of Sam
Story and his family.

Poarch Creek Indian Families of Carolina Cheraw Ancestry

Sizemore, Gibson, Hollinger, Marlow, Durant, Dees

During the resurgence of the Creek identity in the southeast that intensified with the Creek Indian Land Claims cases in the 1950's and peaked in the 1980's, there were many thousands of people doing genealogical work on hundreds of ancestral family lines, many in hopes of finding a Creek ancestors and being part of the land claims settlement awards. For others it was due to actual interest in their own Indian heritage. As a part of the process leading to the federal acknowledgement of the Poarch Band of Creeks, there was a substantial amount of research conducted by various academics as well as countless lay researchers. The Bureau of Acknowledgement and Research within the B.I.A. also delved into the area of the various tribal origins of the ancestors of the modern Poarch Band of Creek Indians. In the course of this researching into the roots of the Poarch Creek community, many ancestors of Poarch Creek Indians were found to have Carolina Cheraw Indian origins. As Poarch Creek Indian researchers, Lou Vickery and Steve Travis state in their book released in 2009 entitled; Rise of the Poarch Band of Creek Indians:

> It is noteworthy that the Sizemore, Gibson, Hollinger, Durant, and Marlow (families), were all mixed-blood lines that came to southwest Alabama from South Carolina. Most were mixed-bloods from the Catawba or Lumbee tribes. – p.144

> The McGhee and Rolin families, along with the Moniacs, Gibsons, and Ehlerts, were the genetic founders of the contemporary Poarch Band of Creek Indians. – p.147

Along with the Dees family, the Hathcocks migrated from South Carolina to the Poarch area where they intermarried with the Poarch Creeks. – p.154

The Hathcocks were originally not Creek Indians. Like the Dees and Gibson familes, the Hathcocks came from the South Carolina area, they were a mixture of Portuguese and Native American, who intermarried with Lumbee Indians. – p.161

William David Bart Gibson was born about 1823 in South Carolina, arriving in Alabama in the early 1840's. – p.154

Listed as a half Creek Indian, (Arthur) Sizemore probably had some Catawba/Lumbee bloodlines. – p. 155

Elaine Hill Fowler gives her granddaughter beads during a traditional Naming (girls coming of age) Ceremony in Blountstown Florida in 2004.

Blountstown Indian Community conference addressed
by Christopher Scott Sewell in 1996

Essie Hill Syfrett and her Children Buck, Lillie Mae, and
Dina along with her granddaughter Teresa Kever attend
Green Corn Dance in Blountstown in 1995

Young warriors, South Arbor;
Tribal Ceremonial Grounds 1995

Appendix

1842 map of Calhoun and Washington Counties FL

Indian Grave house, 1 of 7, Chason Cemetery,
Liberty County Florida 1993

1911 map of Calhoun County, Florida

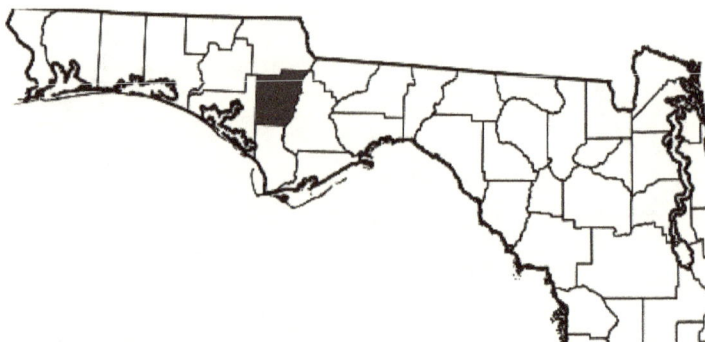

Calhoun County FL, where many Cheraw Indians from the Carolinas migrated to during the 19th and 20th centuries.

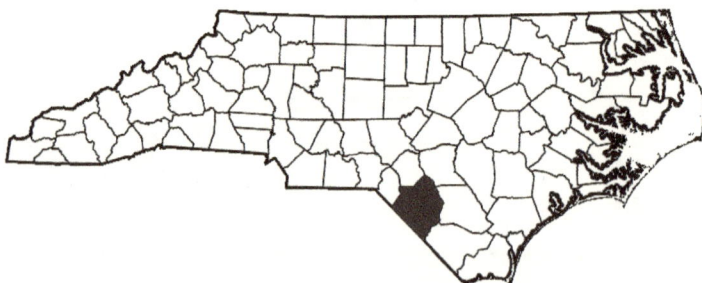

Robeson County, NC where some of these families including Oxendine, Porter, Bass, Jacobs and others migrated from to Florida.

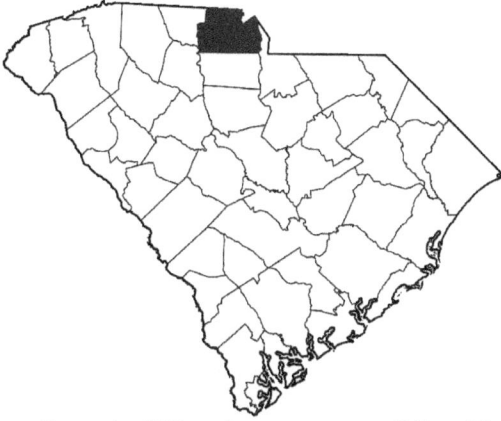

Union County SC, where many of the Florida
Cheraw who were Catawba migrated from to Florida including Scott, Ayers, and others

Absalom Scott
Indian b.SC

Gillatia 'Gilly' Stephens
Indian b.SC
sister of Alexander

Joseph Blanchard
Indian
b. Gates Co. NC

Elizabeth

Samuel Ireland
Indian
b. Maryland

Elizabeth
Indian
b. NC

Rueben G. Blanchard
Served in Confederate
Navy in Civil War

Jane Scott Stone

Samuel Scott
served in Union
Rangers in Civil War

Susan Ireland

John T. Blanchard (SF30)

Ellen Scott(SF31)

- Pearlie Blanchard - married Dock Porter of Scott Town
- Sweety Blanchard (SF32)–married_____ Johnson
  *note: her children were subject of Jackson Co. School case
- Lovey Blanchard (SF33)
- Dovey Blanchard (SF34)
- John Thomas Blanchard (died at 3 years)
- Ella Blanchard (SF36)
- Mary Blanchard(SF37)–married Emmit Dasher of Woods
- Matilda Blanchard (SF38) – married _____ Peacock
- Daisy Blanchard (SF39) – married Corley 'Coy' Scott

(step-son)-------Rufus Jefferson "Jeff" Scott

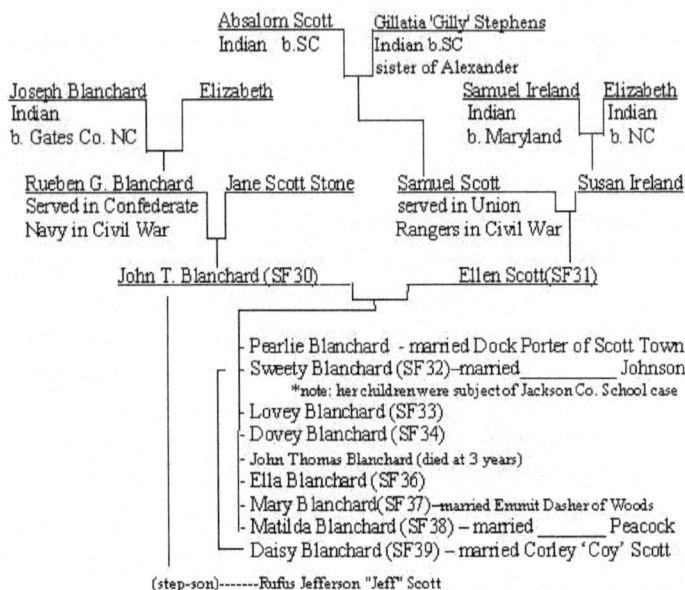

Blanchard Family Geneachart

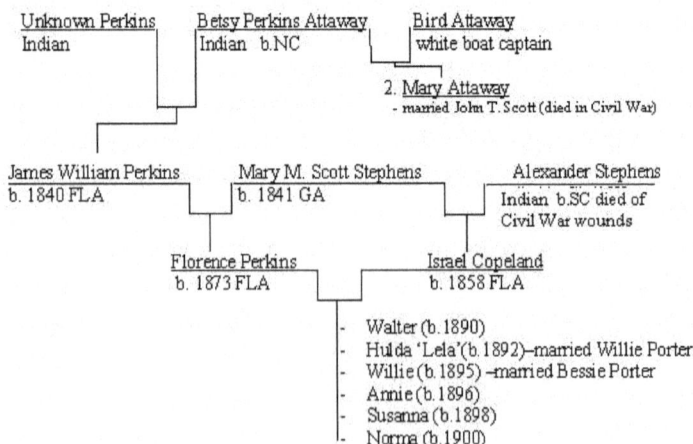

Unknown Perkins
Indian

Betsy Perkins Attaway
Indian b.NC

Bird Attaway
white boat captain

2. Mary Attaway
- married John T. Scott (died in Civil War)

James William Perkins
b. 1840 FLA

Mary M. Scott Stephens
b. 1841 GA

Alexander Stephens
Indian b.SC died of
Civil War wounds

Florence Perkins
b. 1873 FLA

Israel Copeland
b. 1858 FLA

- Walter (b.1890)
- Hulda 'Lela'(b.1892)–married Willie Porter
- Willie (b.1895) –married Bessie Porter
- Annie (b.1896)
- Susanna (b.1898)
- Norma (b.1900)

Betsy Perkins family Geneachart

David Martin 1ˢᵗ
Indian
b. Orange Co. NC

Mary Ann Gibson
Indian
b. Orange Co. NC

Absalom Scott
Indian b. SC

Gillatia 'Gilly'
Stephens
Indian b.SC
sister of
Alexander

David Martin 2ⁿᵈ   Amanda Scott

- James G. Martin (WO11)-married Ella Ayers
- Gillian Martin -married Willie Davis
- Joseph Martin
- Mary J. Martin (SF16)-married 1st Will Johnson 2ⁿᵈ Julius Ash
- Sarah Martin -married G.W. McNealey a Lumbee Indian
- David Martin 3ʳᵈ (SF40) -married Pollie Jones (SF41)

Absalom Scott
ndian b SC

Lillatia
Indian b.SC

Henry Mainer
Indian
b. Sampson Co. NC

Polly Scott
Indian b.SC

Amanda Scott   David Martin 2ⁿᵈ   Beady Mainer   John 'Jack',
Indian
b. Sampson

David Martin 3ʳᵈ (SF40)   Pollie Jones (SF41)

- Dewey Martin (SF42)
- Harvey Martin (SF43) -married Lucille Johns
- Charlie Martin (SF44)
- Leslie Martin (SF45)
- Alex Martin (SF46)
- Bella Martin (SF47) -married Robert McColl
- Ollie V. Martin (SF48)
- Jonas Martin (SF49) -married Jonnie Lee Dav
- Lonia Martin (SF50)
- Willie Martin (SF51) -married Ruby Jones

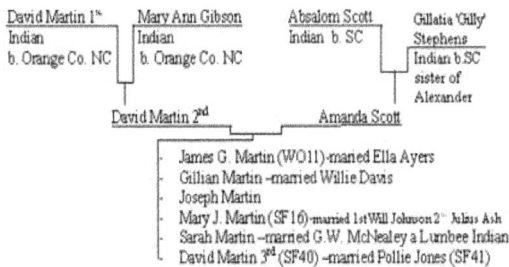

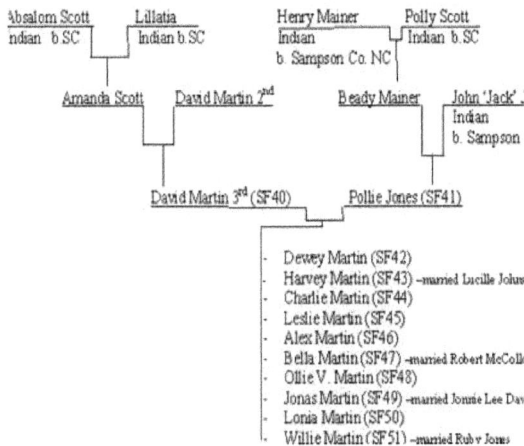

David Martin, Leader of Scotts Ferry Settlement Geneachart

King Hagler
a.k.a. Nopkehe
b. 1710-15
d. 1763

Catawba female

Matthew Toole (white man)

Jenny
b. 1735-45

John Scott

Sally -m- Gen New River
b. 1730-40
d. 1820

1) Gen Jacob Scott (b. 1755-60 d. 1821) became ruler in 1804
2) Billy Scott (b. 1760-65)
3) John Scott (b. 1760-65 d. Robeson Co. NC)
4) David Scott (b. approx 1770 d. Sumter Co. SC)

Gen. Jacob Scott -m- Sally (?)
b. 1755-60   b.1755-60
d. 1821

1) Jacob Scott (b.1790) --m—Betsy Ayers daughter of Gen Jacob Ayers
2) Absolom Scott --m—Ginny Stephens
3) Samuel Scott (b. 1799)
4) Caty/Katy Scott (b. 1799)

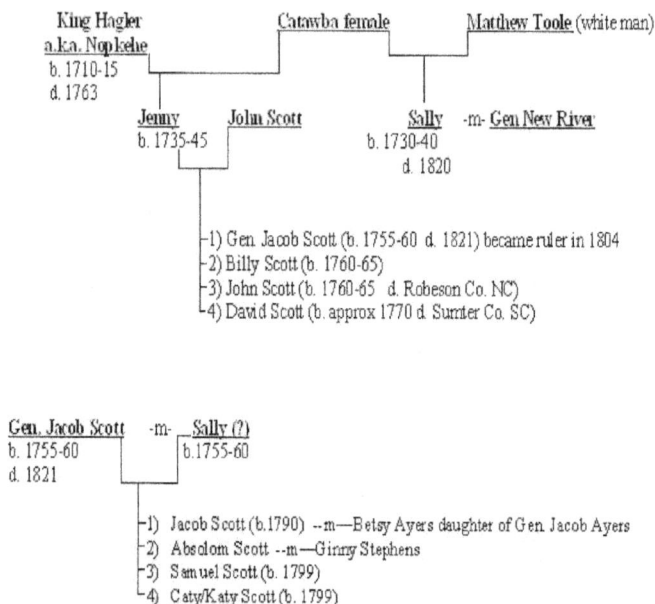

--Sally Newriver was described as an old woman in 1816 by Professor Blackburn.
--Thomas D. Spratt in a letter to Draper in 1871 stated that Sally Newriver & Jenny Scott were ½
sisters and that Gen. Jacob Scott & Billy Scott were grandsons of King Hagler
--Billy Scott & Gen. Jacob Scott both claimed to be grandsons of King Hagler, Brown, Douglas S.,
"The Catawba Indians" 1966

Absalom Scott Geneachart

Bird Attaway   Betsy Perkins Smallwood
White boat captain   Indian b. NC

Absalom Scott   Gillatia 'Gilly'
Indian b.SC   Stephens
SC Militia in   Indian b.SC
Seminole War   sister of
                       Alexander

John T. Scott   Mary Attaway
Died in Civil War

Unknown man   William Ann Scott

- Lula Scott (ST28) – married Beasley Bullard a Lumbee Indian
- Maggie Scott (ST8)
- Samuel "Sandy" Scott (ST16) – married Mary Elena Porter (ST17)
      note: listed as 'Caucasian-Indian' on WWI enlistment
- Thomas F. Scott (ST31) – married Daisy Porter (ST32)
      note: listed as 'Caucasian-Indian' on WWI enlistment
- Kate Scott (ST18) – married _____ Larramore
- Catherine Scott   - lived with Woodie Staley (a Negro)
- James 'Jimmie' Scott
      note: listed as 'Caucasian-Indian' on WWI enlistment
- Willie Ann Scott (ST10)
- Asias Scott (ST11)

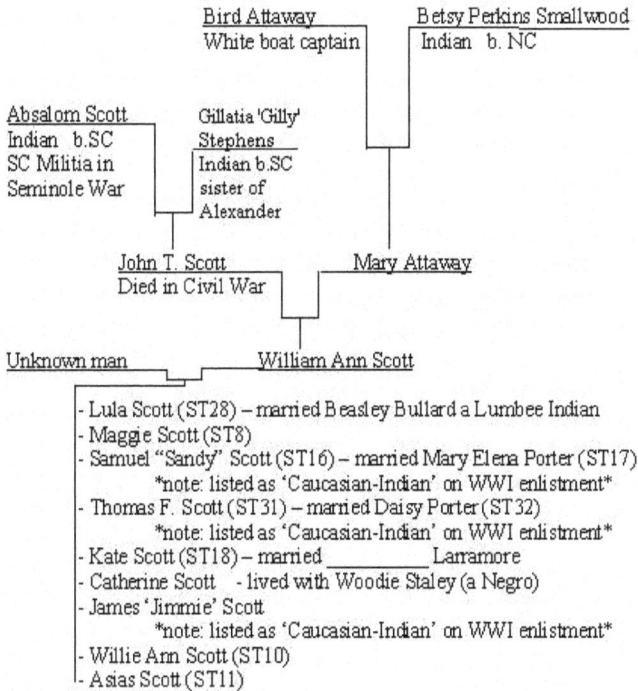

Note: grand-children of William Ann Scott: Jonas Thomas (ST12) born 1905
                                                  Paul Porter (ST13) born 1914
                                                  *attended school at Scotts Ferry
                                                  Loulla Bell Porter (ST14) born 1915
                                                  *attended school at Scotts Ferry

Tom Scott Geneachart

Scotts Ferry School (Colored)
1930-1940 Records

These are the 1930-1940 Calhoun County School records for Scotts Ferry (Marysville/Frink/Cherokee) School, which was funded as a Colored School by the county but which was attended by the Indian children of the settlement. The names of many of the male relatives of the students in the school are identified as Indian on their 1918

WW I Civil Enlistments, court cases, and other collateral documents.

When researching this information, we were rudely refused access to the rest of the school records after the purposes of the inquiry were explained, with the worker saying they were "in too bad of a shape to be handled". We were told this despite our reiteration of our care and of the importance of this project in documenting the history of not only the Indian settlement, but the history of the county and state as well. At this writing the records for the Jackson county school records are mostly gone pre-1930, so we work with what we do have, especially the correspondences concerning Mary Francis Porter and the Cherokee Indian Normal School in Robeson County. The handwriting on the documents were made either at the time of the records creation, or in the cases where "Black School" is written on it, by the person who gave us the records at the Calhoun County Schools Record Office.

> There are men who would knife us out of having our own school saying that we are negroe. You know our character that we are of white and Indian blood. – Scotts Ferry School Trustee Dave Martin to Calhoun County Clerk of Court, 1938.

> Some of the forefathers claim there was no negro blood, but there was Indian blood. This, we are unable to substantiate by any official records. – JD Milton, Superintendent of Jackson County Schools in correspondence upon interviewing Tom Scott of Scott Town as to the community's origins, 1942

Lists of students families by surnames by year

- 1930-31 – Ash, Webb, Hicks, Barnwell, Patterson, Owens, Singleton, Scott, Benjamin, Washington, Martin

- 1931-32 – Scott, Barnwell, Martin, Fisher, Washington, Parker, Porter, Benjamin, Owens, Nelson, Brown, Ash, Wells, Tyson, Britt, Keith

- 1936-37 – Martin, Barnwell, Bird, Gorden, Rainy, Clark, Scott, Smith

- 1937-38 – Brown, Gardner, Martin, Bird, Keith, Small, Williams, Scott, Barnwell

- 1937-38 – Hill, Bennett, Cooley, Holly, Quarterman, Long, Willis, Johnson, Smith, Britt, Sanders

- 1938-39 – Hill, Quarterman, Bennett, Dean, Harley, Jones, Willis, Sanders, Britt

- 1938-39 – Washington, Jones, Martin, Smith, Gordon, Scott

- 1938-39 – Horn, Davis, Paste, Davis, Hill, Gains, Ellis

- 1940-41 – Barnwell, Washington, Baker, Gardner, Martin, Kelly, Allen, Evans

TEACHER'S DAILY REGISTER

BlACK

of

School No. _____ Grade _____ Situated at *Scotts ferry*

County of *Calhoun* Florida

_____ County Superintendent

SCHOOL YEAR 193_1_ - 193_2_

Term Beginning *Sept 22* Ending *May 28*

Olivia Woods Teacher

Supervisor or Trustees

_____ Chairman

_____ Secretary

_____

Issued by
State Superintendent of Public Instruction
Tallahassee, Florida

No.	NAME OF PUPIL (Write ... me first. List boys ... rades, then list girls by grades)	Grade	DATE OF BIRTH Year	Mo.	Day	Date of Entrance	Date of Withdrawl	NAME OF PARENT OR GUARDIAN
	Scott Wesley	3	1914	Aug		7/22/31		Jessie Scott
	Barnwell C. L.	3	1826	Jan	14	7/22/31		Margaret Barn...
	Barnwell Irvin	3	1919	May	1	7/23/31		Margaret Barn...
	Martin Leroy	3	1919	Sept	5	7/22/31		Polly Martin
	Martin Lonnell B.	3	1917	Dec	28	7/22/31		Polly Mart...
	Martin Jonas	2				7/22/31		Polly Martin
	Fisher Eddie	2	1917	Jan	29	7/13/31		Julie Fisher
	Barnwell Florida	2	1921	Sept	14	7/22/31		Margaret Barn...
	Washington Allen	1	1922	Feb	7	7/28/31		Mary Washington
	Barnwell Q. C.	1	1923	June	14	7/24/31		Margaret Barn...
	Fisher Emanuel	1	1918	Dec	2	7/13/31		Julia Fisher
	Scott Bethel	1	1924	Aug	27	7/22/31		Jessie Scott
	Washington Fannie May	5	1918	April	20	7/28/31		Mary Washington
	Parker Robert	4st	1921	Sept	21	7/23/31		Katie Dular...
	La D. Porter	clerk				7/23/31		Florence Wilso...
	Martin Fred	...				7/22/31		Polly Martin
	Martin Alvin	...	1926	March	21	7/22/31		Anna Mart...
	Benjamin Alexander	...				7/28/31		James Benjam...
	Owens John Wesley	...				7/4/31		
	Nelson M. B.	...				8/4/31		
	Brown James	...	1925	Oct	9	8/13/31		Fleta Brown
	Ash Robert	...				8/12/31		Leola Wells
	Wells Jessie May					8/28/31		Leo... Wells
	Tyson Dallisa					8/29/31		
	Nelson Rosa May					8/15/31		
	Owens Mary					8/15/31		
	Britt Bernice					8/15/31		
	Brown Georgia		1923	May	8	8/18/31		Fleta Brown
	Grace Bertha Lee					8/18/31		
	Keith Corine		1927	April	16	8/14/32		Cora Keith
	Keith Lillie May		1925	Nov	9	8/14/32		Cora Keith
	Ella Bell Porter							

Surnames of Listed Students and Parents: Porter, Keith, Brown, Britt, Owens, Nelson, Tyson, Wells, Ash. Martin, Parker, Washington Scott, fisher, Barnwell,

THE PUPILS

1930
Marysville

NO.	NAME	AGE	DATE OF ENTRANCE	PARENT OR GUARDIAN	1st Week
	Robert Ash	6	Aug 25	Leola Webb	
	Jessie Mae Webb	12	" "	" "	
	Maudie Mae Hicks	10	" "	Charlie Hicks	
	J. C. Barnwell	7	" "	Colonel Barnwell	
	Hutchinson H. Patterson	11	" "	Stephen Patterson	
	John W. Owens	6	Aug 27	John Owens	
	Mary Owens	8		John Owens	
	Frank Singleton	6	Aug 27	Lizzie Singleton	
	Frederick Martin		25	Drew Martin	
	Alvin Ruth Martin	9	Sept 2	Dewey Martin	
	Bethel Mae Scott	4	Sept 4	Jeff Scott	
	Haywood Hicks	12	Aug 25	Charlie Hicks	
	Alexander Benjamin	9	" "	James Benjamin	
	Florida Barnwell	8	" "	Colonel Barnwell	
	Wesley Scott	12	Sept 3	Jeff Scott	

Total Attendance for the Month.
Average Attendance for the Month.

Surnames of Students and Parents Listed: Scott, Barnwell, Benjamin, Hicks, Singleton, Owens, Patterson, Webb

NO.	NAME	AGE	DATE OF ENTRANCE	PARENT OR GUARDIAN

Attendance of Teacher.

	Allen Washington	11	aug 25	Allen Washington
	Willie M. Singleton	9	" "	Lizzie Singleton
	Ozela Singleton	11	Aug 26	Lizzie Singleton
—	Leroy Martin	11	" "	David Martin
—	Jonah Martin	13	" "	" "
—	Lonnie B. Martin	12	" "	" "
	C. B. Martin		Sept 1	
	Fannie M. Washington	13	Sept 1	Allen Washington
—	Estella Martin	14	aug 25	David Martin
—	Eulah Barnwell	16	" "	Caleb Barnwell

Total Attendance for the Month,
Average Attendance for the Month.

Surnames Listed: Barnwell, Martin, Washington, Singleton

FLORIDA
TEACHER'S REGISTER OF ATTENDANCE
Small Size
(For 45 pupils or less)

Fourth Edition
1940

(Marysville)

SCHOOL _____ White / Negro SCHOOL No. _____ DISTRICT No. _____

Address _____ County of _____
City or Town   Street or Rural Route

Name of Teacher	Dates Taught		Check Grades or Sections for Which Record is Kept												
	From:	To:	Kgn.	1	2	3	4	5	6	7	8	9	10	11	12

SCHOOL YEAR 19_40_ 19_41_

Beginning _____ and Ending _____

This Register is the property of the county board of public instruction. Each teacher responsible for recording and reporting data on attendance is required to keep the register neatly and accurately according to instructions, make all reports promptly, and return the Register at the close of school to the office of the county superintendent (through the principal) before the teacher's salary for the last month can be drawn. It becomes an important official record for the classroom and the school. PLEASE READ AND FOLLOW DIRECTIONS.

Authorized by
STATE BOARD OF EDUCATION
Tallahassee, Florida

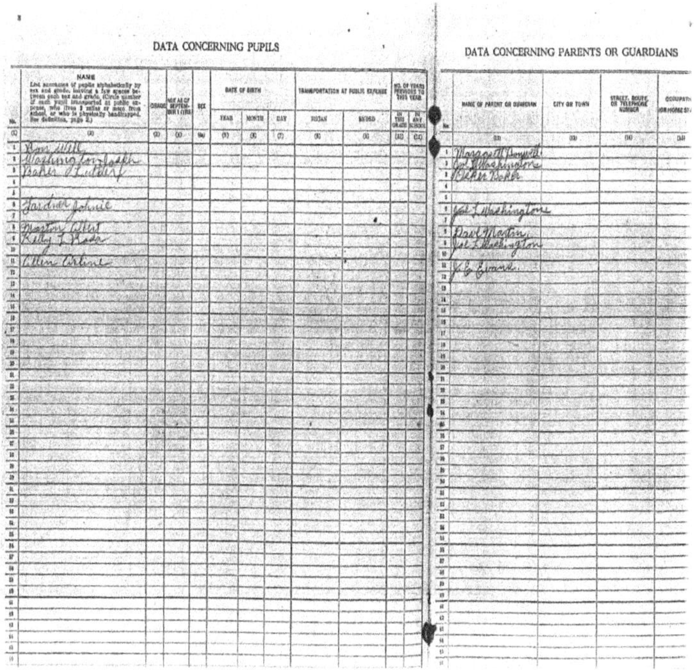

| DATA CONCERNING PUPILS | | | | | | | | | | | DATA CONCERNING PARENTS OR GUARDIANS | | | |

The table is a school register form with the following column groups: NAME, GRADE, AGE, SEX, DATE OF BIRTH (YEAR, MONTH, DAY), TRANSPORTATION AT PUBLIC EXPENSE, NO. OF YEARS, and on the right side NAME OF PARENT OR GUARDIAN, CITY OR TOWN, STREET/ROUTE OR TELEPHONE NUMBER, OCCUPATION.

Handwritten pupil names (left side):
1. Mary Nell
2. Washington, Joseph
3. Baker, Luther
4.
5. Gardner, Johnie
6. Martin, Albert
7. Kelly, J. Rhoda
8.
9. Allen, Arline

Handwritten parent/guardian names (right side):
1. Margaret Barnwell
2. Joe J. Washington
3. Becker Baker
7. Joe J. Washington
8. Paul Martin
9. Joe L. Washington
11. J. C. Barnwell

Surnames Listed: Allen, Kelly, Gardner, Martin, Baker, Washington, Barnwell

FLORIDA
TEACHER'S REGISTER OF ATTENDANCE
Small Size
(For 45 pupils or less)

Second Edition
1938

(Broadbranch)

SCHOOL _____ White / Negro   SCHOOL No. _____ DISTRICT No. _____

Address _____ _____ County of _____
City or Town   Street or Rural Route

Name of Teacher	Dates Taught		Check Grades or Sections for Which Record is Kept											
	From:	To:	Kgn.	1	2	3	4	5	6	7	8	9	10	11	12

SCHOOL YEAR 193_ 193_

Beginning _____ 19__ and Ending _____ 19__

This Register is the property of the county board of public instruction. Each teacher responsible for recording and reporting data on attendance is required to keep the register neatly and accurately according to instructions, make all reports promptly, and return the Register at the close of school to the office of the county superintendent (through the principal) before the teacher's salary for the last month can be drawn. It becomes an important official record for the classroom and the school. PLEASE READ AND FOLLOW DIRECTIONS.

Authorized by
STATE BOARD OF EDUCATION
Tallahassee, Florida
June 9, 1937

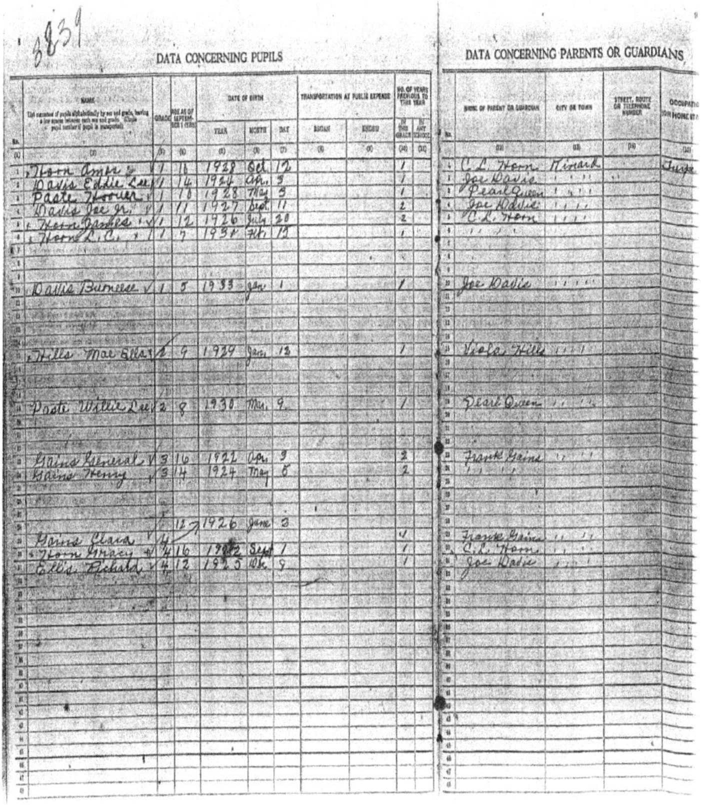

3839

DATA CONCERNING PUPILS

No.	Name	Grade	Age as of September 1 (yrs)	Year of birth	Month	Day	Transportation at public expense: Began	Ended	No. of years previous to this year: In this grade	In any school
1	Horn Amos	1	16	1928	Oct.	12			1	
2	Davis Eddie Lee	1	14	1924	Apr.	5			1	
3	Paste Hoover	1	10	1928	May	3			1	
4	Davis Joe Jr.	1	11	1927	Sept.	11			2	
5	Horn James	1	12	1926	July	20			2	
6	Horn L. C.	1	7	1931	Feb.	13			1	
10	Davis Burnese	1	5	1933	Jan.	1			1	
15	Hills Mae Ella	2	9	1929	Jan.	12			1	
19	Paste Willie Lee	2	8	1930	Mar.	9			1	
23	Gains General	3	16	1922	Apr.	9			2	
24	Gains Henry	3	14	1924	May	6			2	
28			12	1926	June	3				
29	Gains Clara	4							1	
30	Horn Gracy	4	16	1922	Sept.	1			1	
31	Ellis Richard	4	12	1925	Oct.	9			1	

DATA CONCERNING PARENTS OR GUARDIANS

No.	Name of parent or guardian	City or town	Street, route or telephone number	Occupation or home st[…]
1	C. L. Horn	Kinard		Turpe[…]
2	Joe Davis	" "		
3	Pearl Queen	" "		
4	Joe Davis	" "		
5	C. L. Horn	" "		
6	" "			
10	Joe Davis	" "		
15	Viola Hills	" "		
19	Pearl Queen	" "		
23	Frank Gains	" "		
24	" "			
29	Frank Gains	" "		
30	C. L. Horn	" "		
31	Joe Davis	" "		

Surnames Listed: Ellis, Horn, Gains, Paste, Hill, Davis

1751-58

FLORIDA
TEACHER'S REGISTER OF ATTENDANCE
Small Size
(For 45 pupils or less)

First Edition
1937

Marysville

SCHOOL *Ma1z E V171* ~~White~~ SCHOOL No. _____ DISTRICT No. _____
Negro

Address *Blountstown* _____ County of *Calhoun*
City or Town   Street or Rural Route

Name of Teacher	Dates Taught		Check Grades or Sections for Which Record is Kept											
	From:	To:	Kgn.	1	2	3	4	5	6	7	8	9	10	11	12
Florence Goosly				✓		✓	✓		✓	✓	✓				

SCHOOL YEAR 193 7-193 8

Beginning *August 30* and Ending *April 22nd*

This Register is the property of the county board of public instruction. Each teacher responsible for recording and reporting data on attendance is required to keep the register neatly and accurately according to instructions, make all reports promptly, and return the Register at the close of school to the office of the county superintendent before the teacher's salary for the last month can be drawn. It becomes an important official record for the classroom and the school. PLEASE READ AND FOLLOW DIRECTIONS.

Authorised by
STATE BOARD OF EDUCATION
Tallahassee, Florida
June 9, 1937

DATA CONCERNING PUPILS

No.	NAME List surnames of pupils alphabetically by sex and grade, leaving a few spaces between each sex and grade. (Circle pupil number if pupil is transported)	GRADE	AGE AS OF SEPTEMBER 1 (YRS)	DATE OF BIRTH			TRANSPORTATION AT PUBLIC EXPENSE		NO. OF YEARS PREVIOUS TO THIS YEAR	
				YEAR	MONTH	DAY	BEGAN	ENDED	IN THIS GRADE	NOT IN SCHOOL
(1)	(2)	(3)	(4)	(5)	(6)	(7)	(8)	(9)	(10)	(11)
1	Brown, Louis	1								
2	Gordon, Janie B.	1								
3	Martin, Joe Nathan	1								
4										
5										
6										
7	Brown, Lucile	1								
8	Byrd, Clyde Mae	1								
9	Keith, Lillian	1								
10	Keith, Stella	1								
11	Small, Elsie Mae	1								
12										
13										
14										
15	J. D. Byrd	3								
16										
17										
18										
19	Gordon, Mattie Louise	4								
20	Keith, Ada	4								
21	Williams, Sarah D.	4								
22										
23										
24										
25	Martin, Olvin	6								
26										
27										
28										
29	Martin, Fred	7								
30										
31										
32										
33	Scott, Bethel Mae	7								
34										
35										
36										
37	Barnwell, J. Q.	8								
38										
39										
40										
41	Barnwell, Florida	8								
42										
43										
44										
45										
46										
47										
48										

Surnames Listed: Barnwell, Scott, Martin, Williams, Keith, Gordon, Byrd, Small, Brown

TEACHER'S DAILY REGISTER

of

School No. _____ Grade _8_ Situated at _Scotts Ferry_

County of _Calhoun_ Florida

J. K. Musgrove County Superintendent

SCHOOL YEAR 193_6_ 193_7_

Term Beginning _Aug 31_ Ending _April_

Florence Jacoby Teacher

Supervisor or Tr. ___

_____ Chairman

_____ Secretary

David Martin

Issued by
State Superintendent of Public Instruction
Tallahassee, Florida

No.	NAMES OF PUPILS First Half Year Only. (Record names of boys first, leave a few lines, and then record names of girls.)	Grade	DATE OF BIRTH		Date of Entrance	Date of Withdrawal	GENERAL DATA CON NAME OF PARENT OR GUARDIAN
			1878 Mo.	Day			
1	Leroy Martin	8					Martin
2	Luril Martin	5	1926 Nov 21		Aug 31		Martin
3	C. Barnwell	7			Aug 31		Barnwell
4	W. Byrd	2			Aug 31		Byrd
5	Fred Martin	6			Aug 31		Martin
6	B. Gordon	1					Gordon
7	Frank Rainy	4					Rainy
1	Oma M. Gordon	4			Aug 31		Gordon
2	Mattie M. Gordon	5			Sep 31		Gordon
3	Rosa Lee Clark	7			Sep 31		Clark
4	Lillie May Hogan	1			Sep 31		Hogan
5	Elandy Mae Byrd	1					Byrd
6	Bethel Mae Scott	6					
7	Florida Barnwell	7					
8	Ader Keith	4	Feb 8				
9	Lillian Keith	1	Feb 23				
10	Estell Keith	1	Feb 23				

Surnames Listed: Keith, Barnwell, Scott, Byrd, Clark, Gordon, Rainy, Martin

FLORIDA
TEACHER'S REGISTER OF ATTENDANCE
Small Size
(For 45 pupils or less)

Second Edition
1938

(Marysville)?

SCHOOL _____   White / Negro   SCHOOL No. _____   DISTRICT No. _____

Address _____   County of _____
City or Town.   Street or Rural Route

Name of Teacher	Dates Taught		Check Grades or Sections for Which Record is Kept											
	From:	To:	Kgn.	1	2	3	4	5	6	7	8	9	10	11	12
					✓✓		✓			✓✓					

SCHOOL YEAR 193_ 193_

Beginning _____ and Ending _____

This Register is the property of the county board of public instruction. Each teacher responsible for recording and reporting data on attendance is required to keep the register neatly and accurately according to instructions, make all reports promptly, and return the Register at the close of school to the office of the county superintendent (through the principal) before the teacher's salary for the last month can be drawn. It becomes an important official record for the classroom and the school. PLEASE READ AND FOLLOW DIRECTIONS.

Authorized by
STATE BOARD OF EDUCATION
Tallahassee, Florida
June 9, 1937

of Monthly h.
Preparing
along with s.

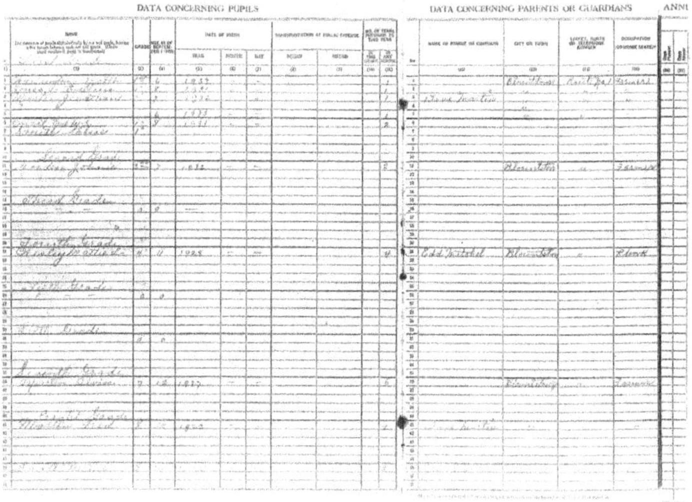
DATA CONCERNING PUPILS

DATA CONCERNING PARENTS OR GUARDIANS

ANN

Surnames Listed: Martin, Wesley, Gordon, Smith, Washington

FLORIDA
TEACHER'S REGISTER OF ATTENDANCE
Small Size
(For 45 pupils or less)

Second Edition
1938

SCHOOL _Frink_   ~~White~~ Negro   SCHOOL No. _____   DISTRICT No. _9_

Address _Frink, Fla._   _R. R._ County of _Calhoun_
City or Town   Street or Rural Route

Name of Teacher	Dates Taught		Check Grades or Sections for Which Record is Kept												
	From:	To:	Kgn.	1	2	3	4	5	6	7	8	9	10	11	12
				✓	✓		✓	✓	✓						

SCHOOL YEAR 1938. 1937.

Beginning _August_ _29th_ and Ending _April 21st_ _1939_

This Register is the property of the county board of public instruction. Each teacher responsible for recording and reporting data on attendance is required to keep the register neatly and accurately according to instructions, make all reports promptly, and return the Register at the close of school to the office of the county superintendent (through the principal) before the teacher's salary for the last month can be drawn. It becomes an important official record for the classroom and the school. PLEASE READ AND FOLLOW DIRECTIONS.

Authorized by
STATE BOARD OF EDUCATION
Tallahassee, Florida
June 9, 1937

Surnames Listed: Britt, Sanders, Jones, Dean, Harley, Willis, Bennett, Quarterman, Hill

Surnames Listed: Sanders, Cooley, Long, Hill, Johnson, Wright, Smith, Dean, Bennett, Willis, Hill, Quarterman

𝕭ackintyme

30 Medford Drive
Palm Coast FL 32137-2504
860-468-9631

To order extra copies of this book, visit
http://backintyme.com/ad375.php

Our complete line of publications is at:
http://backintyme.com/publishing.php